I Should Have Known

Memories of a Gay Married Man

By Dean Gardner Ostrum

For John – all the best always!

Dean Gardner Ostrum

I Should Have Known

Memories of a Gay Married Man

By Dean Gardner Ostrum

Originally published by Dijau Press – New York

Burnin' Media Publishing - New York

I Should Have Known - Memories of a Gay Married Man

By Dean Gardner Ostrum

Hard Cover by Dijau Press – New York 2007

Paperback by Burnin' Media Publishing, NY, NY. 2011

PRINTED IN THE UNITED STATES OF AMERICA

Ostrum, Dean Gardner.

I Should Have Known - Memories of a Gay Married Man

1. Lawyers & Judges – Bio/AutoBio 2. Gay & Lesbian – Bio/AutoBio 3. Cultural Heritage – Bio/AutoBio 4. Personal Memoirs – Bio/AutoBio

Library of Congress Control Number: 2011938097

ISBN: 978-0-9792989-5-0 Softcover

DEDICATION

For my parents, Helen and Oscar Ostrum, who taught respect for all people—regardless of race, religion, or sexual orientation.

Dean sniffing petunias

CONTENTS

INTRODUCTION

"*Y*ou are the most selfish and egotistical boy I've ever met!"

That's what my friend Lucille New once told me when we were Junior High School classmates in the tiny prairie town of Russell, Kansas. I felt bad and it hurt me terribly—not so much because she'd said it, but because I had the guilty feeling she might be right.

I've always wanted people to like me. If she'd just said "selfloving and self-confident" it might have been a compliment, but it most certainly wasn't. To this day I can still hear the distasteful tone of voice she used in giving me her opinion.

Why then am I writing these memoirs? Aren't such things occasioned by people who just want to brag or who somehow believe that their life stories will be fascinating to others? Perhaps. But I like to believe that I'm writing, first because my oldest son John has repeatedly encouraged it, and second because I'm hopeful that my writing may be helpful to others willing to listen.

Events over which I have had no control have shaped large parts of my life, and decisions I have consciously made have determined most of the rest. As I near my eighty-fourth birthday and still enjoy the blessings of excellent health, each new day becomes important and I feel an obligation to spend it in useful ways.

For more than thirty-six years I was married to a wonderful woman whom I still love. Our marriage was fruitful – blessed with four fine children, a girl and three boys. We now have nine grandchildren, five boys and four girls, two great granddaughters and one great grandson. Sari, my still beautiful former wife, and I visit often and are on friendly terms. I have recently completed thirty-one years of living with Richard, a man who is twenty years my junior.

I'm gay. In retrospect I probably should have known from the time I was five. Except for the pain my gayness has unquestionably caused my wife and children, I have absolutely no regrets. I have come to believe that my sexual identity is just as much a gift from God as life itself. This then is my story. No doubt each of my loved ones would tell it differently.

Therefore, dear reader, please keep in mind what Lucille said. You will be reading the memoirs of the most selfish and egotistical boy she ever met. You may find it of interest to know that we remained good friends for the remainder of her life, a life that ended far too soon from a cancer she was unable to conquer. I guess I'm still egotistical enough to believe that before she died she found me not so selfish.

Discovering one's true sexual identity probably never happens like a bolt from the blue. At least for me it was a gradual thing. Should I have known earlier on? Probably not—but suspected, most certainly yes.

"If Grandpa Dean is gay, why did he ever marry Grandma Sari?"

That was the question my son Danny's daughter Sari asked her father when she was about eleven.

"Well," he replied, "if he hadn't, you wouldn't be here, would you?" That was the end of the conversation.

When my oldest grandson Jason first broached the subject with his mother, my daughter Karna, he was about the same age. The two of them were alone in the bedroom of our New York City apartment where she was ironing a dress for his younger sister Betsy.

"Do Grandpa and Richard have just one bed?" he asked.

"Yes," she replied.

"Do they sleep together?"

"Yes."

"Are they gay?"

"Yes."

"Oh," he simply answered, no longer curious and apparently completely satisfied.

Soon afterwards and before all five of us left for dinner my daughter called me aside on our terrace and whispered, "It finally happened," repeating their brief exchange. That evening, and to this day, I have noticed no difference in the loving relationship Jason and I have. For him the knowledge was a nonevent.

In looking through the many snapshots in the baby book my mother carefully kept during my early childhood years I was always intrigued by a photo taken of me sitting on the front porch of our two-story frame house in tiny (population 2,500) Russell, Kansas. It was 1927 and I was just five years old, soon to start kindergarten. The photo appears on the cover of this book. I'm sniffing petunias. Should I have known?

CHAPTER ONE: Outed by my children

*T*hinking back, I realize I had inklings of my sexual orientation as early as five, certainly by twelve. Never once did I play doctor with the neighbor girls, but it was ever so exciting that hot summer morning Dick Woods and I showed each other our bare bottoms in the vacant field of tall weeds and sunflowers behind his house.

Feelings of greater sexual interest began in junior high school gym class, especially when we wrestled or stripped to go to the showers. Half-erections were common and the first guy to sprout a little pubic hair was kidded unmercifully. Things heated up considerably one sultry morning the following summer when an older boy, Billy Marshall, and I were making stew in my backyard to earn our merit badges in cooking. Aware that I had noticed his more than ample endowment protruding from his Boy Scout shorts, he grinned a sheepish grin and offered to show me something *really* interesting if I'd follow him into our garage.

There I witnessed my first lesson in masturbation (having been told nothing about this strange phenomenon by either my parents or my older brother). Rather quickly Billy proudly demonstrated his ability to "cum". Never shy, he repeated this feat for me almost every day for several months in his family's bathroom. An eager and admiring voyeur, I watched and suffered in silence until the night of my first wet dream. What a relief to discover that I wasn't different. Eager to show Billy that mine worked too, I was quickly dismayed when my friend told me that such childish things were now beneath him. He was in love, he said, and regularly "screwing his girl."

During the late thirties in high school I always had a girl myself and double-dated frequently. There was lots of heavy petting, but in those days the good girls seldom permitted intercourse. Frightened by movies about venereal disease that were shown in health class, cautioned always by my mother to treat my dates as sisters, and absolutely panicked by the thought of knocking someone up, I turned for my sexual life (other than self-gratification) to two high school buddies and mutual masturbation. One of these buddies was an accomplished musician who later became a celebrated pianist in a Kansas City night-club. The other was a star high school athlete who later went to Notre Dame, lettered in varsity baseball, got married and fathered six sons.

My first sexual encounters with other boys my age or slightly older occurred when I was in junior high and high school. Though dating and enjoying the company of girls, I faithfully followed my mother's advice to treat them as I would a sister. Sexual experiences with boys continued in college – occasional masturbation with a few fraternity brothers, but never with my closest college friend (later to be best man at my wedding, and I at his) Bob Stewart. Our sleeping porch at the fraternity house was unheated and the double-decker double beds required that most of us be assigned a bedmate. College girls at that time had the objective of remaining virgins until marriage and a guy's raging hormones often found an outlet with other guys – most of whom were heterosexual.

After a succession of girl friends I finally met a strikingly beautiful girl named Sarepta Mable Pierpont, thoughtfully knick-named Sari by her younger brother. A music major and gifted violinist, she played first chair second violin in our splendid university orchestra. There was lots of competition getting dates with Sari and at first I had to settle for quick coke dates before and after rehearsals. Being a bass clarinetist in our university band, I enjoyed the novelty of carrying her violin case around the campus and felt particularly right with her when she became the first woman ever to tell me I was a good dancer.

Soon we were seeing each other frequently and she invited me to her home in Chanute, Kansas, to meet her parents and two brothers. They were great people, whom I liked immediately. Life for us was joyous and carefree with fraternity and sorority parties, a lot of class and lab work, and even an occasional weekend beer bust with my later-to-be-best-man, Bob Stewart.

Then came Pearl Harbor.

Radio news of the Japanese bombing interrupted a lazy Sunday brunch at my fraternity house, and life changed. As a sophomore R.O.T.C. student I enlisted in the U.S. Army Infantry Reserves. Here today, gone tomorrow, was the feeling pervading our young lives – and it proved tragically prophetic for scores of our friends. Pinnings (the gift of your frat pin to your girl) increased in number, and whirlwind marriages and departures for military service became common occurrences. Summer school with uninterrupted military training was now required of all reservists.

One warm, moonlit night the following summer Sari and I were making out in the upper row of seats in the empty football stadium and I asked her if she would take my fraternity pin. As if it were yesterday I remember her startling answer.

"You know what this means, don't you? It means you're asking me to marry you."

I had only intended to ask her to go steady – that is, to date only me as long as she kept my pin. Slightly embarrassed, but knowing that I'd never had another girl as wonderful as she, I allowed as how she was right. It really did seem like a good idea and that's how I got engaged. In a manner of speaking my future wife proposed to me, but I have never regretted it.

In the spring of 1943 I was called to active duty, later commissioned a Second Lieutenant in the U.S. Army Tank Destroyer Corps, and soon thereafter assigned to the Seventh Armored Division in Fort Benning, Georgia.

On December 25, 1943, Sari and I were married in a beautiful church in Birmingham, Alabama. It was still decorated for Christmas. The only attendants were the minister, Sari's parents, the kindly old black janitor who lit the candles, and my best man Bob Stewart – by then a handsome young U.S. Navy Reservist headed for medical school. At a two-man bachelor party the previous night, Bob and I had exchanged uniforms, a court martial offense if ever there was one, and made the bar rounds as a farewell to my life as a single man.

After only weeks of married life together (her parents had understandably insisted as a condition of our marriage that she complete her last semester of college) I shipped out of New York harbor aboard the Queen Mary on D-day. Later, going ashore on Omaha Beach my division spearheaded the breakthrough in Normandy at St. Lô – beginning eight months of combat in France, Belgium, Holland, Luxembourg, and Germany.

Following the end of the European war I had my first sexual encounter since being married – with an army officer. Without having met us before, he had asked my colleague and me to share drinks in his hotel room. A general's aide and graduate of Princeton, he seemed to me to have no motive beyond extending hospitality as we passed through Augsberg, Germany, on our way back to Leipzig. My older companion, an army major, was tired from our travels and begged to be excused. I was happy to accept since good Scotch was hard to come by and my monthly ration was long gone.

As we proceeded to get rather drunk together in his room, the topic of conversation eventually turned to boyhood sex and my newly married status. Suddenly he asked if I had ever experienced oral or anal sex with a guy. I answered no and he immediately offered me the option. I was happy to accept. I chose a blow-job. It was fantastic and I felt no shame. Almost all the other men I knew in my outfit, many even married, had been shacking up with girls – English, French, Belgian, Dutch and German – ever since we first arrived overseas. For me, however, this was the first sexual betrayal of my married life.

Upon returning home months later from Germany I thought of telling my wife of the experience in Augsberg, but was afraid of her reaction and chose to be silent. Though sex with my wife was exciting and enjoyable, I found myself fantasizing about men and desperately lonely whenever she indicated unwillingness for intercourse. In every other way our life together was interesting and mutually rewarding. I had re-entered college, and when I graduated I went on to Yale Law School. Soon we began our family, the first two of four – a wonderful little girl and boy, in that order, both born in New Haven.

For almost four years I resisted frequent opportunities to act on my desires. But then came the Korean War with a recall to military duty and months of separation from my wife. Unable any longer to resist the growing temptation, I finally gave in. Off and on, with months and sometime years in between, I lived a double life until my children brought me out.

One quiet Sunday morning in New York City in 1977 after we'd made love in the studio apartment I kept in the Village, my wife of thirty-four years suddenly said, "I have a question for you. Your boys would like to know if Richard is your lover."

Stunned by being confronted with my homosexuality after what to me had been a very happy marriage, I responded in the negative. Being a lawyer, I rationalized my answer by thinking, "Yes we have sex, but no, we're not lovers in the sense that word is used in the gay community."

Immediately, I felt devastated. I had lied and I knew it, but dear Sari didn't press the subject further. Several years earlier, again following intercourse, she had asked me if I was bi-sexual. I remember replying that I was and guessed I always had been. But the next logical question – Do you ever have sex with men? – never came.

I was in the closet and my wife shared that closet with me. Both of us were afraid to break the silence. Possibly that was the reason she had said "your boys," and not "I want to know."

When later that afternoon Sari left in her car for our home in New Jersey, I rode with her as far as the entrance to the Holland Tunnel. When I got out and said good-bye, my world was collapsing around me.

I was being outed by my children. What would happen next? For the first time in my life I thought (briefly) of suicide.

How had my children known?

Upon reflection it was obvious. For three years I had never kept Richard, my closest and dearest friend in the city, a secret. And neither was my family a secret to him. In the event of emergency his name and telephone number were prominently displayed on a slip of paper under a refrigerator magnet in the kitchen in New Jersey. I talked of him often and his Christmas and birthday gifts to me had not been inexpensive.

In addition my children were by then young adults, either in college or beginning their careers. They had gay friends; and they had been brought up in a home that taught respect for diversity, be it racial, religious, or sexual. Simply stated, they weren't naive. It was only I who mistakenly believed that I was so discrete that no one would ever suspect – short of catching me in the act.

Fortunately a letter arrived the next day from my youngest son, Peter. It afforded me a second chance to tell the truth, but more important, an opportunity to leave the closet. It was Peter's first letter to me following our family Christmas vacation and read in part as follows:

> ...The time we spent together in New York really felt good. But at the same time I can feel a change in both you and Mom. Not only am I concerned about you as my father but as my friend. I have come to grips with the fact that Richard is probably your lover. I don't feel bad or hurt at this fact for you have taught me well & raised me to understand these things and accept people as they are. Don't falsely judge people. These ideals that you have instilled in me are probably the greatest things anybody has ever taught me, and I hope to instill them in my children. As my parents, Sari and you must come to some agreement, before you destroy each other. Decide

> what is best for you as individuals ...Regardless of what happens, I will still love you as my friend and as my father, both for whom I have the utmost respect...I can only speculate on how you must feel and what you're going through. My heart goes out to you. We are all so afraid and alone, it's time we crushed these wicked walls of silence and put down this heavy load.

Overjoyed and relieved, I answered Pete immediately – acknowledging the truth of my gayness and my relationship with Richard. I quickly posted my reply in the nearest mailbox. Not trusting the mail I called my son that evening to tell him of my response and thank him for his help.

The next months were consumed with personal visits to each of our four children to answer any question that might concern or even interest them. All were curious about the time I first thought I was different and why I had married. The conversations were intimate and uninhibited.

Divorced, but never remarried, my former wife remains my close and loving friend. She has made great progress in forgiveness and acceptance of a gay person's inability to change. Though her Christian Science religion teaches her otherwise, I hope and believe she finally realizes that our sexuality is not something we choose. It's unquestionably a gift of nature – a gift from God some say.

My children, I believe, are proud of the length of my relationship with Richard, now thirty-two years and growing stronger as time passes. He is a part of our family and accepted by everyone. All of us have many gay friends, business associates and several other gay relatives as we've now learned.

As bell hooks, the brilliant black writer, observed in the final words of her moving essay "Talking Back," *Moving from silence into speech is...a gesture...that heals, that makes new life and new growth possible.*

It has certainly been true for me, and I trust as well for my family and Richard.

CHAPTER TWO: Then and Now

In many ways my life used to be a rat race; now it's more peaceful and serene. Richard and I live in a penthouse paradise of trees and fountains in the heart of Greenwich Village, with a breathtaking, panoramic view of downtown, uptown, and the broad expanse of the Hudson River. Sunsets can be spectacular and the river traffic is fascinating – colorful tugboats, beautiful sailboats, huge cruise ships and occasionally the grand, yet clunky, new Queen Mary 2 that replaced the sleek, elegantly designed QE 2. Sadly the downtown view no longer includes the Trade Towers, but eventually the even taller Freedom Tower will replace them.

One might think that the change in my life came when I retired from a high-pressure job as a corporate attorney. Not so. It came after admitting to my wife and children that I was gay – that there was an integral part of me I couldn't change. It came from getting honest.

Like most gray-flannel suited men of my generation I was driven by the desire to make good, to earn more money every year for my growing family, to live in a better house, to drive a more expensive car, to receive another promotion, to rise higher on the corporate organization chart, and very possibly in my particular case to prove to my sports-loving father that I didn't have to be an athlete to be successful.

On reflection, it's likely that I was powered by a desire to prove my masculinity.

For almost my entire adult life before coming out I was subconsciously aware, indeed I was fearful, that I might suddenly die (a plane crash, a car wreck) and later my family would somehow learn the big secret. Perhaps finding a stash of gay magazines, or by the posthumous receipt of a letter to me from a former lover, they would learn that their son, husband, father, friend had been a homosexual. The tragedy would be that I would not have had an opportunity to explain, to tell my side of the story.

As it turned out, because my children outed me, I got my chance and my immediate family was amazingly understanding and accepting. The sole exception was my sister-in-law, my only brother's wife.

Idabelle seemed horrified. "Whatever you do, Dean," she counseled, "don't tell your mother. It would kill her."

And I did, but it didn't.

It still makes me smile when I recall how it happened. It was Christmas and I had come home alone to Kansas to visit my mother, the first time without my family. She was over ninety years old, spry and alert.

"Dean, honey," she said the first evening, after we had finished the supper dishes and she was comfortably seated without her apron in my late father's favorite old brown leather recliner in her immaculate living room. "Are you and Sari having some kind of difficulty? There's something about her letters now that tell me something's wrong."

I acknowledged that there was a problem, and she immediately asked, "Is there another woman?" Assuring her that there wasn't, I quickly moved the conversation on to a different topic.

The next night, after we had washed and dried our few dishes and were again seated in her living room, she continued her inquiry, as if no time whatsoever had intervened.

Taking my hand in both of hers, she simply and sweetly asked, "Dean, are you homosexual?"

When I told her I was, that I always had been, she assured me that it didn't matter in the least, that she loved me dearly, and that she thought Richard, whom she'd corresponded with after receiving birthday cards for several years, seemed like a wonderful person.

Contrary to my sister-in-law's prophecy of death, she seemed relieved to know the truth about my marital problem and ended by asking the next logical question. "But what do you do?" This time I was less responsive, suggesting that she use her imagination.

Sometime before that special evening I had run across an old photo of my mother taken when she was eighteen. She was surrounded by three attractive older girls, arms entwined, smiling pleasantly for the camera. On the back of the photograph was the inscription: "The B.G.N.B.N.B.B.C. Club, Dec. 19th, 1906". When I asked what those initials stood for and whether I could have the photo, she said that I could and that it was just a little club that she and some of her schoolteachers belonged to.

"And the initials?" I asked.

"Bachelor Girls Not By Necessity But By Choice," she replied.

That photo, together with one of my father at eighteen with his raggedly-dressed Bethany College scrub football team, now hangs in a place of prominence in our New York City apartment. And that night's coming out to my mother afforded me the opportunity to ask another question regarding my father that I hoped she might answer, he having died eight years previously.

"How do you think Daddy would have reacted to the news of my gayness?"

"Well there's no doubt whatsoever." she hastened to assure me. "His feelings would have been no different from mine. We love you and your brother without reservation; we just want you to be happy."

Wow! I liked that a lot. It made me even happier than I already was. Since I'd never gone out for varsity athletics – something I knew my father was almost fanatically enthusiastic about – I'd always felt a little guilty (though I knew my mother was pleased, still not wanting her baby to get hurt).

At high school basketball games Okas (as the grandchildren later called him) yelled louder than the cheerleaders, noisily beating the palm of his hand with his rolled-up Salina Journal like a mad man. At high school football games he charted every play of every game, running up and down the sidelines until the day he was tackled and my mother insisted he stop. But the teams loved it and he was always asked by the coaches to speak at their annual award banquets. I never attended (my interests lying elsewhere – in music, dramatics, speech, debate, and student government), but I secretly wished I could have.

Never once, however, do I remember feeling that my father was anything but proud of my accomplishments. He came to my plays, concerts, speech contests, and debate tournaments, and congratulated me with a hearty handshake, a warm smile, and words of encouragement.

Later in life, when my father was in his late seventies, one day as we were saying good-bye following one of my annual visits home from some distant city where I worked, my mother noticed after her embrace that my father and I were formally shaking hands.

"Why don't you hug Daddy, Dean?" she encouraged me. "He would love that."

I did, he did back, and we both loved it. From then on, we always hugged each other when we met or parted. So why is it that men, particularly in America, are so afraid of showing affection, so afraid of loving other men? I believe it has to do with our obsessive search for masculinity. We are taught as children that men must be strong, implying that it's okay for women to be weak; that men must be the breadwinners (the providers), and that their wives are there to make a home for the family, to bear and care for the children, and to be sexually available to their macho-posturing husbands.

In my case a perfect example was the pique and unhappiness I felt when my wife once got a part-time job working in a department store in Cleveland. It made me feel less than a man, less of the provider and protector. It meant a sharing of responsibility in an area of masculine life that I thought should be reserved for the stronger sex.

Rubbish! In truth, my reluctance to show weakness and my excessive drive to compete, to excel, to conquer in whatever I undertook had to do with proving myself a man.

I now know that I am a man, always have been, and that I'm completely comfortable being gay. Just as the women's movement in the world has succeeded in freeing many women from male oppression, the movement for gay liberation has made amazing progress in freeing men from homophobia.

Ola and Mary Ostrum family portrait with seven of their eleven children (Oscar, Dean's father, top right)

Boyhood playmate Dick, Dean, Charles and brother Will

The rascals – Dean, Dick, Charles and Will

CHAPTER THREE: Growing Up Years

According to my baby book, Dean Gardner Ostrum was born at 5:20 a.m. on January 2, 1922, in his parents' home at 32 Fossil Street, Russell, Kansas. Weight 8 pounds. No length recorded. Tellingly perhaps, the listed baby gifts include "embroidered dress," "white kid shoes," "pink and white booties," and a "rubber dog."

An entry under the heading "First Ride" reads, "Taken to St. Anthony's Hospital at Hays, Ks. for an operation – cause being hernia – Dean lacked a few days of being 8 weeks of age – Dr. Jameson of Hays operated – in the hospital 2 weeks."

This event had unusual significance in my growing up years because it meant that rough sports were discouraged. I can still hear my mother cautioning, "Now whatever you do, don't overdo." Her first pregnancy had resulted in a stillborn baby girl and she often spoke of how very painful the births of my brother and me had been for her. Much of her concern could probably be traced to a family tragedy that occurred only months prior to my parents' marriage on November 26, 1914. Her only brother, Walter Gross, had lost both his wife Clara and their baby son Kenneth in childbirth.

Growing up in Russell, a small town in west central Kansas, during the twenties and early thirties was in many ways idyllic. (Not so idyllic was the Great Depression and the horrendous dust storms that took place during that period.) I had loving parents and wonderful grandparents. My mother's parents, called Poppa and Mama, lived in Bunker Hill, a much smaller town just ten miles away. My dad's parents, who had immigrated to America from Sweden, also lived in Bunker Hill but his father Ola Ostrum had died before I was born and I have but a fleeting memory of my grandmother Mary Ostrum.

Another entry in my baby book, under the heading "Favorite Pets," is "Dogs" – capitalized and heavily underlined, followed by the name Doodles. This dog belonged to our farmer milkman, Mr. Shaffner. It was Mr. Shaffner who made me a gift of my first of many dogs, a fox terrier named Babs.

In those days milk was whole milk, not pasteurized, straight from the cows and packaged in glass quart bottles that had to be washed and returned to the farmer when he came with his next delivery. Besides the milkman, we also had an iceman, who delivered huge blocks of ice during the summer months. When he arrived all the neighborhood kids would congregate around the back of his wagon. There were often spoils when he used his ice pick to cut the smaller blocks. He carried the blocks with ice tongs to our icebox – no electric refrigerators in those days. Always friendly, he would reward us with small hunks of ice that we wrapped in rags to suck on. How great that small piece of ice felt in your mouth when the temperature was about 100 degrees and sometimes even as high as 110 to 115.

In those days we had no TV weather channel to tell us what the heat index, humidity level, or feels-like temperature was. We knew, however, that summers in Kansas were hot, hot, HOT. As a special treat when visiting my grandparents in Bunker Hill during summer, I was occasionally given a nickel for an ice cream cone (always chocolate). Walking the two short blocks to the drug store soda fountain and passing the blacksmith shop where sweating, bare-chested men hammered out horseshoes on their anvils was especially exciting to me.

One particularly hot day I was visiting an older boy, Jack Eberly, who lived along old Highway 40 to the east edge of my parents' house. Jack was quite an entrepreneur, with his very own rabbit and pigeon business. People ate rabbit meat (it tastes really good) and squabs (about the size of a Cornish game hen – also delicious). From time to time Jack let me help feed and water his charges and clean their cages.

On the day in question the temperature must have reached 120. There was no breeze of any kind and by noon the poor rabbits were on their sides struggling to breathe. Their hutches were extremely heavy and we worked as fast as we could to move them from the open barnyard to the shade of a few Chinese elm trees near the Eberly house. Jack was beside himself with concern for his rabbits and I got to hear a string of swear words I'd never known existed. At the end of the day we had a few dead rabbits, but the pigeons weathered through.

One of the swear words I heard but had no idea what it meant was "FUCK, FUCK, FUCK!!!" Later that fall I saw the same word scrawled on the wall of an abandoned shed across from the grade school. I knew it must be something bad, but never had the courage to ask anyone what it meant. Parents in those days didn't discuss the subject of sex with their children. On the other hand my parents were never shy about nudity. I saw both my parents naked at times after bathing or when they were dressing, and thought nothing of it. To their credit this allowed me to grow up with no sense whatsoever that our private parts were in any way dirty or shameful. It likewise pleases me to observe that my children seem to have reared their children with the same respect for their bodies.

Photos from my baby book bring back very pleasant memories – my own sand pile, my first bike (really a tricycle). Like many children I was in love with my kindergarten teacher, Miss Leach. My only sibling, brother Wilber (eventually shortened to Will) was three years older than I. Accordingly I was not included in his circle of friends and felt a little left out.

Our only cousin on my mother's side was her only sister Ethel's daughter and only child Helen Georgina Humes. Being two years older than Will and quite plump when a little girl, she too treated me like a kid. One day in our home in Russell when I was alone in the bathtub, the two of them looked in on me through the keyhole. When I heard them laughing, being a bit of a voyeur myself, I stood up naked and draped the wet washcloth over my then erect penis.

Visits to Helen's home in Ponca City, Oklahoma, were always highlights of those early years. Her father was a pharmacist and owned a drugstore where we were always treated to chocolate malts at their soda fountain. Her mother was my favorite aunt. She told off-color jokes, drank cocktails, always brought a box of Mrs. Stover's Chocolates when she visited us, and tragically died when only sixty years of age.

Other trips we took outside of Russell County were a few drives to Kansas City, stopping in Abilene along the way. Our car had frequent flat tires and the roads were mostly gravel. At one garage stop for car repairs I was so completely fascinated looking at a poster of a carload of people entering a railroad crossing in front of an oncoming train, that I failed to follow my parents and brother as they walked up the street to look around the town. The panic I felt when I found myself alone and abandoned was overwhelming. I began to cry and an eternity later – though only minutes, they returned to my rescue. Later in life, as a prisoner of the Germans during World War II, I suffered a similar feeling of being abandoned, but I didn't cry.

The most important person during my growing up years was always my mother, and even after leaving home for college, for war, for marriage and for rearing my own family, I telephoned her frequently and corresponded with her often. When she died at one hundred and two years of age a lengthy obituary appeared in the Russell newspaper. Nothing I could write tells a better story of my family in those early years.

OBITUARY Editor's Note: Helen Ostrum, lifelong resident of Russell County, died Nov.13, 1989, at the age of 102. Following is the obituary on Mrs. Ostrum as given by her family. The obituary is followed by a feature on
Mrs. Ostrum published in the Hill City Times about 12 years ago.

Helen Ostrum, daughter of Daniel and Kate (Gardner) Gross, was born on November 11, 1887, in Bunker Hill, Kansas. She passed away peacefully on November 13, 1989, at the Russell Regional Hospital in Russell, Kansas, at the age of 102 years and two days.

On November 26, 1914, she was married to Oscar Ostrum and they had two sons, Wilbur and Dean. Their entire married life was spent in Russell where Oscar maintained an active law practice until shortly before his death on April 24, 1969.

Modestly describing herself as "just a homemaker all my life," Helen assisted and supported Oscar in their many church, civic and community activities, including the Trinity United Methodist Church, the Eastern Star and Masonic Lodge, the Russell Board of Education and the City Council, the Russell Rotary Club, the Bethany College Alumni Association and the County, State and American Bar Associations.

Following Oscar's passing, Helen continued to maintain her home in Russell, living alone, surrounded by her many loving neighbors. She suffered a stroke in May of 1988, recovered her speech, never lost her mental faculties and sweet smile, but remained in the Respite Care Program at the hospital until her death.

Her last eighteen months were spent with her roommate and cherished friend of over 70 years, Irene Hupfer. She had frequent visits from her family and friends, with care from a hospital staff that she continued to praise, saying simply, "They couldn't be better."

Helen is survived by her loving sons, Wilbur and Dean; her daughters-in-law, Idabelle and Sari; seven grandchildren Karna, John, Danny, Peter, Stan, Lisa and Kris; five great-grandchildren, Jason, Betsy, Cody, Sari and Anders; her niece Helen Humes

> Johnston; her sister-in-law, Belva Ostrum; her dear friends, Gertrude Iden, Norma Mundy, Richard Nagrodsky, the former Brooks girls, Frances, Ruth and Virginia, Viola Rowe, Bertha May and Leo Dwinelle, Kathryn St. Aubyn, Anita Dole, Josie Sellens, Fern Hollinger, Faye Hedges, and her many other loving neighbors and friends.

The article from the Hill City Times reads in part as follows.

> ...The Farmers and Merchants Bank is proud to recognize another northwest Kansan who has achieved the nine decade mark in her service to her community and state. Rating our plaudits at this time is Mrs. Oscar (Helen Gross) Ostrum of Russell, Kansas.

...Helen Ostrum was born the daughter of Daniel and Kate Gross at Bunker Hill, Kansas, on November 11, 1887. Her father operated the general store in that eastern Russell County town for "many, many years" and the building is still standing just across the street west of the well-known Bunker Hill Restaurant.

"I worked in that store, and never got very far away from Bunker Hill for any length of time. We sold everything in the store and I did quite a little bookkeeping for my father," Helen said. She was one of three children in the Gross family.

The Russell woman went to school in a two-room school with two teachers and remembers that it was a full-day trip to Russell to the dentist in the family horse and buggy. "We never wanted for something to do," she said, adding that friends got together frequently, with many activities centering around the Lutheran Church to which the family belonged. "Young people were working constantly in the church," she said.

Speaking of the family's first phone, Helen commented, "What a treat! Now we have every convenience possible in our homes. We wouldn't want our children to have it like we had it back then; we can be thankful for the changes!"

Noting that the young people at the turn of the century in Bunker Hill "Walked everywhere they went," Helen remembered particularly fondly the winter months spent at the pond near the town. "I never learned to skate; I was the one who was always down."

Helen's life has centered around her home and her husband, Oscar Ostrum, who was born November 26, 1884, and was a school mate of hers. Oscar graduated from Bethany College, which he attended while Helen stayed home, and the couple were married on November 26, 1914, Oscar's birthday and Thanksgiving Day, in the Gross home in Bunker Hill.

The young couple moved to Russell, where Oscar had a job as a court reporter and he studied law under an attorney there. After taking and passing the bar examination, Oscar joined Lyman Beardsley in his Russell County legal practice.

While Oscar served for fifteen years as the Superintendent of the Sunday School at his Russell church and enjoyed games of all kinds ("Oscar loved chess!"), Helen noted that, "I just took care of things at home. After my father's death, my mother made her home with us as she was almost blind, so we had that added responsibility."

The couple had two sons: Wilbur is an accountant with Texaco in Houston, Texas, and he and his wife, Idabelle, have three children, Stan, Lisa and Kris. The other son, Dean, is a vice-president with Western Electric in New York City and he has four children: Karna, John, Danny and Peter. Helen also counts three great-grandchildren.

A late 1950's trip to the west coast by the Ostrums was interrupted by Oscar's first heart attack, but it wasn't until twelve years later, in 1968, that death claimed the Russell attorney. He announced his retirement from active practice in February and passed away on April 24. "We were so thankful that Oscar could carry on as long as he did," said Helen. "We were able to celebrate over 50 years of married life together and he practiced law up almost until his death."

"I do miss my church work and am now inactive in the Trinity Methodist Church, but I try to keep up the best I can on school activities, etc. I enjoy reading our newspaper, listening to the radio and TV and I have some really good neighbors, who share their news with me and check up on me frequently."

A fall at her home at 443 East Fourth Street earlier this year left Helen with a broken wrist, but mid-December found her "nearly good as new". "It certainly is a fast, fast time that we are living in," she said. "But I certainly wouldn't change a thing from the way things have been to the life I am living now," said the very pleasant, attractive Russell woman.

CHAPTER FOUR:

My Love Affair With Dogs

After retiring from 36 years of law practice I found great joy in doing many things for which I'd previously not had time – hospice volunteering, studying for and becoming a professional calligrapher, and acting. I eventually got all my union cards (Equity, SAG, AFTRA) and as a Screen Actors Guild Book Pal have spent many years reading to children in the public schools of New York City. The kids call me Grandpa Dean.

One spring my first grade children at P.S. 11 in Chelsea were learning about memoirs and were assigned the task of writing a few words about a simple memory they might have. Their teacher, Chantal Gregoire, asked if I would write an example for the next class, rather than reading out loud from a book.

Following is the memoir I wrote and then read, showing pictures as I went along.

> I'm going to tell you what I remember about the first dog I ever owned. She was a fox terrier, white with brown ears, and her name was Babs. A farmer who delivered milk to my family gave her to me when I was just starting kindergarten. Here's a picture of me with my kindergarten teacher, Miss Leach. As you can see I'm much, much younger than I am now. I was five years old. I'm proud to be posing with my teacher because I'm secretly in love with her. (See photo.)
>
> My family lived in a small town in Kansas. I mean really small, only two thousand or so people. There were no supermarkets, no malls, no movie house, and Main Street was only three short blocks of stores. We

didn't have television, only an old radio. We had no refrigerators, only iceboxes, and milk and ice were delivered to our homes. Before automobiles were invented the milkman and iceman came in wagons drawn by horses. I had an older brother, Will, and no sisters. Here are a couple pictures of me with my brother and our two best friends, Charles and Dick, who lived across the street from us. (See photos.)

In the wagon picture I'm the little guy in the middle. My brother is standing holding the wagon tongue or handle. The older boys are all wearing caps with visors. Being youngest, I'm still decked out in a stupid kid's hat. In the second picture we're standing on the steps of the house in which I was born. My buddy Dick is whispering something to me. I don't remember what he was saying, but you can tell it must have interested me a lot. Dick's brother Charles is the one with the big ears and my brother is the guy with the tough, gangster look on his face.

Even though I might have been the smallest of this gang of four, I was actually the luckiest because I would later be the first to have my very own dog. Being the youngest, most of the other things I got were hand-me-downs from my brother. And speaking of that, here's a picture of me and my first bike. It was a tricycle and I found this photo in my old baby book.

You guessed it. It used to be my brother's. You can tell two things if you look carefully. First, I'm pretty proud of it. Second, I've grown up a bit since the wagon photo. Can you see my visor cap on the ground beside me?

Incidentally, I also found in my baby book the following notation under the item Favorite Pets: "DOGS. Will love any kind of a dog." It's in my mother's handwriting, just like the notation under the bike photo.

Now, let's get back to the subject of my first dog. In a memoir I find that it's easy to wander when you're writing. Just like when you're talking. One thing suggests another and before you know it you're off on a subject that has little to do with what you started with.

At that time in my life this dog was the most wonderful thing that had ever happened to me.

Would you believe that my mother even let Babs sleep in the same bed with me at night? Winters in Kansas got awfully cold. Although we slept between flannel sheets with lots of covers, it still felt mighty good to have a warm puppy beside you – and often right in your arms. Here's a picture of me with Babs when she was a puppy. (See photo page) I regret that I have no photos of her as she grew older. Babs never had a leash like a city dog. There weren't any laws about picking up dog poop, probably because in a little town there weren't a lot of people to step in it.

Babs was well trained, and this proved to be her downfall. She could sit up and beg for food, roll over on command, and whenever I whistled she came immediately. She followed me everywhere I went. The only time we were separated was when I went to school. Kindergarten wasn't bad because I was gone only half a day.

Summers were the very best. With no school we went everywhere together. We played outdoors. She loved my sand pile. She got a little nervous when I climbed up high into the old maple tree beside our house. We were inseparable.

And that was the way it was until one fateful day in September of my first year in Second Grade. It was a wonderful sunny afternoon. My friend Dick and I had just come home from school. As was our custom we went to play in the large vacant lot behind our houses. The lot was overgrown with weeds and we had made neat tunnels through the heavy grass. In those days there were no interstate freeways and just a narrow two-lane highway (U.S. 40) that ran on one side of this huge lot where we played.

When it came time for supper Dick's mother called out from their back porch, as she always did, that it was time to stop our play and return home. I noticed that Babs was not in sight as we started to leave. I climbed up on a large pile of rocks that had been cleared from the field and began to whistle. As I turned my head toward the highway I saw Babs across the road pricking up her ears to look at me. She hesitated a minute and then bounded toward us. But just as she got to the edge of the road a large truck came barreling down the highway. Her mind was on obeying my whistle and she failed to look before crossing.

You all know what happened next. I ran to the road and found my beautiful Babsie lying quietly along the side of the ditch. I guess the truck driver hadn't felt the impact, he was long gone. She looked like she was asleep. There were no marks on her small white body, but a little trickle of blood was seeping out the nostrils of her tiny black nose. I lifted her limp little body into my arms and hurried home. At least she'd been killed instantly. My heart was broken.

That evening I wrapped her in a white towel, placed her in a cardboard box, and buried her in our back yard. Later I found a large oval-shaped sandstone rock, carved her name on it and placed it on her grave.

People often say it takes at least a year to get over the loss of a loved one. I learned early in my life that they are right. Every night that winter I took Babs' little brown collar to bed with me. It still had her dog tag on it and the leather smelled just like her. I can remember many days in Second Grade when my thoughts would turn to my dog. My eyes would fill with tears, but I could never tell my teacher what was bothering me. I think my parents did however. She sometimes made an excuse to come by my desk and put her hand on my shoulder. I think I eventually came to love her, too, but never as much as Miss Leach.

One day the next summer the farmer who had given me Babs brought a new puppy to our back door when he delivered the milk. We named her Sheila. She, too, was a fox terrier – maybe with the same parents.

I've had a lifetime love affair with dogs. Even today when I walk along the New York City streets and see a dog on its leash coming toward me, I get a warm feeling in my heart. Usually the dog and I make eye contact, the tail wags, and I feel like I'm looking at an old friend. For every one I have had in my life I could write another chapter in this memoir. Maybe someday I will.

While I can't have a dog conveniently in New York right now, I do go to California occasionally to visit the beautiful Border Collies of friends. The last photo shows me holding Lucy and Mattie right after we flew them back to San Francisco from Southern California. They love to herd sheep. If you remember seeing the movie Babe you'll know what wonderful dogs the Border Collies can be.

From the experience of having Babs, what did I learn? At least three things. Having a pet is a rewarding experience. Losing a pet hurts a lot. And finally, getting a new one is often the quickest way to get over your loss.

That was the end of the memoir I read to the children that spring.

Since then I've continued to read to at least one first grade class every Friday morning during the school year. Each spring the teachers ask me to read the chapter book Charlie and the Chocolate Factory. They then show the children the movie Willie Wonka & the Chocolate Factory and each class develops questions about how certain things happened, principally special effects. My youngest son Peter Ostrum, who played Charlie Bucket (the good boy in the movie), later comes down from upstate New York where he's a veterinarian and speaks to the class. (Filmed in Munich, Germany, over more than four months, it was the only movie

Peter ever made. He loved doing professional theater as a child, but found movie making too disruptive to his life and turned down a contract for more films.)

One day I was sitting at the back of a subway car in New York City traveling down to the Village from the upper west side. When the train stopped at the Museum of Natural History station an entire class of twenty-some children boarded with their chaperones and teacher. They were second graders and two little black boys sat down next to me. The boys then got on their knees to look out the window. A chaperone saw that one of them had his shoe up against my jacket and cautioned him to sit back down. At that moment he looked me in the eye and then screamed down the length of the subway car to the other children, "GRANDPA DEAN. GRANDPA DEAN IS HERE."

Immediately it was bedlam. All the other children, boys and girls, began making their way back to my seat. What a reunion. The train eventually reached the Twenty-third Street station and all disembarked for Public School 11.

"Are you some kind of celebrity?" a young man across the aisle from me inquired as the train left.

"No," I replied. "They're just a class of children I read to as a Screen Actors Guild book pal."

The young man told me he was attending New York University and majoring in film. When he eventually gets his SAG card, I have a feeling he may be volunteering for our book pal program.

CHAPTER FIVE: Contributing To Equality

Is it possible that my being gay has had something to do with my lifelong feeling of empathy with black people? Or saying it another way, has my minority status in a predominately straight society made me more aware of how unfair it is to let racial, religious, or sexual difference stand in the way of seeing any person as being as wonderful as any other? Possibly so, but more likely it has been the result of my upbringing.

Early in my childhood my parents taught me that prejudices were wrong. My father was a small-town country lawyer whose parents had been poor Swedish immigrants to America. He had a lucrative practice with several clients who became quite wealthy when oil was discovered in Russell County, but he also represented many poor people without charge. Many of his clients were blacks who lived in surrounding counties as well as our own. Dad died suddenly of a heart attack when he was eighty-four. His funeral packed the Trinity Methodist Church he had helped build and there were many black families in attendance. A memorial tribute to my father, written by one of his competitors, Marvin Thompson, is evidence of his professionalism, fairness and deep concern for his clients. (See Appendix #l.)

In those early days people of African descent were forbidden even to stay overnight in many towns in Kansas—nearby Hays for example. (Nicodemus, a very small town near Hill City in northwest Kansas was populated solely by blacks.) In our little town of Russell there were only two black families— the Sowells and the Cookseys. I was surprised and saddened when I learned that on out-of-town football and basketball games Warren Cooksey, one of our school's best athletes, had to have his meals brought out from the cafe to the school bus while his white teammates ate together inside.

Later, in college, my then girlfriend and later-to-be-wife Sari told me of the same kind of discrimination that her friend, a black violinist, had to endure when the University Symphony Orchestra traveled to Kansas City. It was not until after World War II that black students at KU began lunch counter sit-ins in an effort to end this demeaning treatment. In those years sororities and fraternities were segregated and many had rules forbidding integration.

During World War II I saw firsthand how blacks were totally segregated from white troops. Most were in the Quartermaster Corps driving trucks and bringing in supplies, but their officers were white. Racial segregation in our country's military didn't change until President Harry Truman issued an executive order ending it prior to the Korean War in 1950.

In June of 1953, following my defeat by Bob Dole the previous fall in our primary race for Russell County Attorney, I accepted appointment as an Assistant Attorney General of Kansas. This required that my family, now consisting of my wife and our first three children, move to Topeka. It was there that the First Assistant Paul E. Wilson asked me to read and comment on his brief in what later became the landmark United States Supreme Court decision unanimously finding racial segregation unconstitutional – Brown vs. Board of Education. The then Attorney General Harold R. Fatzer had assigned Paul the politically unpopular task of arguing the case for the State of Kansas – the Topeka Board of Education being the defendant.

Years later Paul wrote about this experience and consistent with both of our strong feelings at the time he entitled his book A Time to Lose. (University of Kansas Press 1995) In the fly-leaf appears "Ecclesiastes 3:8: To every thing there is a season..." For anyone interested in reading a sensitive, yet shockingly accurate, account of what a Negro's

life was like in the 1940's, Paul's writing is in my opinion unsurpassed. Can you
even begin to imagine what black children in Topeka must have thought when they learned that the municipal swimming pool was only open for them one day in the spring and that the pool was then completely drained and refilled before whites could use it? Our time in Topeka was less than a year. In early 1954 I accepted an offer from Southwestern Bell Telephone and we moved to St. Louis where I began a thirty-one year career in corporate law with the Bell System. Had I known that this career would involve being admitted to practice in seven states and taking four more bar exams, I might have hesitated. As it turned out I thoroughly enjoyed working within the Bell System, particularly because this regulated monopoly encouraged its employees to be active in civic affairs of their choice. As promotions came my way we moved first to Dallas, then New York, again Dallas, then Portland, Oregon, later Seattle, then Cleveland and finally back to New York.

When we moved to Cleveland in 1964 there were no black lawyers in the entire Bell System and none in any of the large Cleveland law firms. Determined to give black lawyers work, I sought the help of my black Yale Law School friend Leon Higginbotham, then a prominent federal judge in Philadelphia, to put together a list of prospective hires. Leon gave me many names of talented black lawyers to interview and opened doors in Washington where I might meet and interview others. The end result of my effort was that I hired several wonderful black lawyers for my department, setting a precedent for similar hiring at AT&T, and was later asked to share my list of prospective hires with the managing partner of one of Cleveland's large law firms.

Years later my middle son Danny's high school soccer classmate John Scott, then a practicing lawyer in the District of Columbia, sent him an article about me, written by the president of the District of Columbia Bar Association. (See

Appendix #2.) It was obvious she had never met me, but her predecessor was one of the black lawyers hired by AT&T. Though I was never a golfer and always a lawyer who traveled in blue jeans and not in 3-piece suits, this article is otherwise an accurate account of my effort to give black lawyers opportunity in the field of corporate and large firm law practice.

While I was in Cleveland, Carl B. Stokes was elected Mayor – the first black to lead a large American city. I had chaired a committee for the Welfare Association studying the problem of youth gang group formation, both black and white, and welcomed anything that might improve race relations in our city. The Watts riot in Los Angeles and the Hough area race riots in Cleveland following Dr. King's assassination prompted President Lyndon Johnson to ask every large American city to form a Mayor's Council on Youth Opportunity. In January of 1968 Mayor Stokes, whom I had never met, called me and asked that I be his chairman. Although my corporate job was demanding, I accepted this challenge with the blessing of my boss, Ohio Bell's president.

The Cleveland's Mayor's Council had more than fifty members representing a broad spectrum – labor leaders, business leaders, professionals, clergymen, educators, and students. One of our youngest members was a black young man who had been one of the Hough rioters. He attended several of our meetings until one day I learned that he had been hospitalized. On my way to work the next morning I visited his hospital bed to bring him flowers and wish him well. He seemed surprised and was obviously pleased to see me.

As his beautiful brown eyes filled with tears, he said, "Nobody ain't never brought me flowers before."

I had noticed that he limped as he walked and I now discovered that this hospitalization was required for the partial amputation of a foot. When a young child his feet had frozen because his home had had no heat and he developed gangrene.

The Mayor's Council had a professional staff—Seymour Slavin being its first Youth Coordinator, later followed by Walter Beach, a former Cleveland Browns professional football player who was black. With funds raised through a community program called Cleveland Now, our goal was to provide summer work and entertainment for underprivileged young people regardless of race.

All was going well until a shootout between blacks and police occurred on July 23, 1968. Six black civilians and three white police officers were killed. The event became known as The Glenville Shootout. It occurred at the site of one of the summer employment programs that had been part of a larger package approved by the Council. A lawsuit by the wounded police and the next of kin of those who had died was later filed against Mayor Stokes, myself, and the Mayor's Council. The suit sought millions in damages. The plaintiff's lawyers theorized that we should have known that money earned by youth in summer jobs might be used to buy guns and ammunition that might later be used to injure or kill policemen. Though termed frivolous by the large, respected Cleveland law firm that volunteered its services in our defense, this lawsuit hung over my head for many years. After giving a deposition in New York City, I eventually had to return to Cleveland to testify before a jury. The trial judge directed a verdict in our favor; the case was unsuccessfully appealed by the plaintiffs; and years later the Supreme Court of the United States refused the case on certiorari.

On the evening following the Glenville Shootout, Sari and I were guests at a dinner party at the home of our friends Bobbie and Alan Geismer in Shaker Heights. The tragedy was on all our minds and I had only that morning appeared with Mayor Stokes before a battery of microphones and television cameras, answering questions from the press. My spirits weren't high to say the least, but two weeks later they were lifted considerably when a column by Adele Silver, a dear friend of the Geismer's, appeared in the Cleveland Plain Dealer. (See Appendix #3) The following words from this article were of particular comfort to me.

> The slings and arrows that have recently been aimed at the Mayor's Council on Youth Opportunity, which operates under "Cleveland Now", could, through public misunderstanding and distrust, jeopardize the intelligent and hopeful plans – to say nothing of the money – that went into the Council's programs. Like a lot of other public committees, the Mayor's Council is attacked from one side as 'a bunch of soft headed dogooders' and from the other as 'fat cat Establishment types.' ....Candor is a polite term for the blunt, sometimes harsh and bruising exchanges I listened to at planning sessions during the spring at Hiram House Camp. Under the patient and generous-spirited leadership of Dean Ostrum, chairman of the Council, those rough talk sessions bore real fruit. Not enough fruit yet – and no one recognizes that more keenly than Mr. Ostrum. Of the inner city's estimated 58,000 kids, probably only about 35,000 were served this summer. One high-risk project has already come to grief. There will be other setbacks and disappointments in others. I hope Mr. Ostrum's 54 fat cats, do-gooders and young rebels will stick it out – for the sake of all of us."

Carl Stokes died on April 3, 1996 at 68 years of age. I remember him fondly and will always be proud to have known him.

CHAPTER SIX: Looking Back

I'm aware that procrastination in finishing these memoirs must stop. Summer before last Helen Humes Johnston, my only cousin on my mother's side, died at age 86 in Oklahoma. I was the only surviving relative to attend her funeral. Though in excellent health and honestly expecting to live at least as long as my mother did, I do live in New York City where taxis routinely run red lights and where only last week a speeding delivery bicyclist going the wrong way on a one-way street brushed my jacket sleeve as he raced by. Could the time for me to finish be coming to a close?

Let me get to work.

To my surprise, I recently learned that my wife had saved every letter I had written her in the many years we were apart during World War II and Korea. After some hesitation she eventually allowed me to read them. (Although dear Sari wrote often to me it was impossible to save her wonderfully welcome letters while in combat. And it disappointed her to later learn that many of my letters had been written at one sitting, backdating them much like a diary.) I was clearly in love and while in Europe wrote frequently of my desire to have children. While in Korea I continued to write of my desire to try for a sister for our daughter Karna and even set four as the number of children I hoped we'd someday have. When I asked her for copies of my letters she graciously consented to having one of my grandsons make computer disks of all of them. And what an experience it has been. To read them is like living those years over again. Here are a few examples.

12 September 1944
My darling Sari,

Today brought two letters from you and four from the folks, but in none of them had either of you received any of my mail as yet. I can't understand why you haven't, unless it was lost or destroyed on the way back. In a Stars & Stripes of the 8th of Sept. received today I see where General Patton has finally announced that the 7th Armored Division is in his army and fighting. Naturally as it was an Associated Press article you have all read it long before now so censorship can't forbid my telling you. It's fairly hot today, but our nights are real cold. I sure would rather spend the night with you, dearest, than the way in which we have to. Everybody's joints get plenty stiff from sleeping in damp foxholes all night. I sleep so soundly as far as shelling is concerned that I'm afraid I might not wake up should a few come our way at night, so I play safe as does everybody else – and dig my hole big enough to get a bedroll in. Don't worry for a minute, darling, about the Captain or myself regarding French women. In the first place we don't have any time & in the second place I sure hope you trust me more than to suspect me of being unfaithful ever to you, honey…Darling, sweet dreams & take care of yourself… It's really night time here now. I'm finishing this in our half-track by flashlight (blackout of course). I go on guard at 5:30 (last shift) tonight so my sleep I'm hoping won't be too much interrupted. I'm living for the day we can be together again, my darling. You're the most wonderful girl I've ever known or could possibly meet. Sweet dreams. All my love, Dean

22 September 1944 France
My darling Sari,
Honey, it has been ages since I've had a chance to write & this can only be a note. I guess back home you may not be able to understand how it could be impossible to write, but believe me it has been. I'll tell you all about it – if you want to hear – when I'm home, honey.
I'm well, tired & homesick for you, darling... Dearest, just to see you again is going to be all of the heaven I'll ever want. Being so far away & with all that goes on around me, I

almost get frightened to know what all has got to happen before we're together again. Never fear for a moment, my sweetheart, we will be together again, though I know that at least in our thought we have never known separation . . . I love you my dearest darling, Sweet dreams. Dean

8 October 1944 Somewhere in Holland
My darling Sari,
Here it is a peaceful(?) Sunday morning in Holland & I wonder what my 'baby's' doing back at home. I got up early (as usual) & heated some water (about a quart) & washed my hair, face & hands for a change. I also shaved & if it wasn't that my combat pants and jacket are filthy, I'd look fairly presentable. These combat suits are all wool-lined & have a million zippers – even a handy side gadget off the front. How do you like that? We sort of look like ski-troopers, but they're warm and it looks like we'll need all we can get on. Battalion maintenance welded a new silver bar on my helmet this morning so I'm all set – even look like a First Lt. now. Gee, honey, it's good not to be just a 2nd John anymore... Thanks for the lock of hair. I think it's getting darker, don't you? I'll cut a whack out of mine & send you. It's sort of dirty but honey it's been through a lot. I know I've gotten older looking – but then like everyone always has said – I could stand it. I got myself a new submachine gun to carry instead of my carbine this morning ...I love you my darling sugarfoot.
Forever yours, Dean
PS Enclosed is one of the safe conduct certificates our planes drop on German lines – some blew back our way.

23 November 1944 Somewhere in Holland
My dearest darling Sari,
This is a cloudy Thanksgiving Day, honey, and as usual it's drizzling rain outside. We're set up very well at the moment – billeted in homes for a change & several of us even have beds to sleep in. The Dutch have been swell to us & we have made ourselves at home, too, as much as possible. Today the

Colonel had the staff sit down to a real table together for dinner. We had a tablecloth, real dishes & silverware, a bouquet of chrysanthemums & even place cards. Our radio goes with us also, so it really was an occasion we'll never forget. We ate turkey, dressing, peas, bread & butter (white bread & real country butter – not canned), sweet potatoes & coffee. In fact we even had a couple Scotch and sodas before dinner. It was plenty touching after all we've been through together. Major Frazier proposed the toast – 'To the 48th Armored Infantry Battalion – and many more Happy Thanksgivings.' It made me sort of get a lump in my throat to think of all the swell men & officers that are no longer with us & never will be again. My first meal I ever ate with the 48th was Thanksgiving dinner in 1943 when I joined the Division last year, so it meant more than you might think. Many is the time, honey, when we were together at Infantry Officers' parties last spring that I wondered if we'd ever actually get to combat as a unit. There's surely no question now, is there? ...Oh, darling, how I love you... Sometimes I think I'll go batty before I can be with you again... By the way, honey, I got an award that I'm plenty proud of the other day – it's the 'Combat Infantryman's Badge'... At least I'll have some medals & ribbons to wear the next time we go out again, darling... Well, sweetheart, I've got a lot of people waiting to see me & a lot of work to do. Take care of yourself, beautiful, & write your sugarfoot often. I love you. Dean"

I always enjoyed intercourse with my wife right up to the one year required abstinence before a no fault divorce could be granted. (In compliance with New Jersey law we refrained from having sex after I was served with her petition.) And only once during our marriage did I even attempt to have sex with another woman. That experience occurred in Germany, some months after the war in Europe had ended, while I was stationed in Heidelberg awaiting assignment to the States. Agnes was a displaced person whose Jewish parents had perished in a concentration camp during the Holocaust. Her looks reminded me of Sari. On our one and only date we began to make out in my hotel room after I had taken her to dinner. She said "No!" to going forward and my one attempt at unfaithfulness with the opposite sex ended with premature ejaculation in my military issue boxer shorts as I kissed her goodbye at the door.

Already related in these memoirs is the encounter with a fellow officer who gave me my first oral sex in Augsburg, Germany, after we killed off a bottle of Scotch in his hotel room. A similar oral experience with a married ex-Marine occurred in Russell, Kansas prior to my re-call to active duty in the Korean War. Neither of these events seemed too meaningful at the time. But following my return to the States in January, 1952, and my unsuccessful run for Russell County Attorney against my high school friend Bob Dole that September, another sexual experience occurred that profoundly affected me.

At Yale Law School, studying for third year exams in half a Quonset hut near the Yale Bowl was often difficult, and close friends who attended Sari's church offered to let me study in one of the bedrooms of their two sons whenever I wished. Both sons were away in the Air Force and college and the quiet was perfect for concentration. I vividly remember my first meeting with Brian (not his real name), the older son, before leaving New Haven following graduation. He was tall, blonde, and slender – a varsity swimmer in college and a devotee of the local YMCA – a real charmer.

Several years later, in the spring of 1953, my growing family and I were living in a small two-bedroom house in Russell, Kansas, where I was practicing law with my father. We were expecting our third child within the month. Having stayed close with Brian we were delighted to receive a telephone call from him saying he was coming through Kansas from Denver and that he wanted to spend the night with us. That evening after our meal together, Sari graciously insisted that Brian sleep with me in our bedroom. She moved to the double-decker bed in the children's room and we all said goodnight.

No king or queen size beds in those days. It was next to impossible for two grown men not to be in occasional contact with their bedmate. We were dressed only in our shorts, and I was soon aware of my own mounting erection. No words were spoken and I finally drifted off to sleep. To my surprise – and delight – I was later awakened with Brian's mouth on my penis as he kneeled, now naked, on the bed between my thighs. Nothing was said the next morning and our guest went on his way to Kansas City. I had no regret or shame whatsoever and accepted what had happened as a natural extension of our friendship. From that night on I would remember and be thankful to Brian for showing me that sex with a man is in no way sordid, but natural and fulfilling.

Later he married a sorority sister of my wife. Because his brother was away in service he asked me to be best man at his wedding. As far as I know his marriage was a happy one with several children. After that special night in Kansas Brian and I had only two brief sexual encounters – once while sitting together in my car awaiting his departing train's arrival in Topeka, and years later in my Brown Palace Hotel room in Denver on a business trip. Brian is no longer living and I sometimes wonder what other experiences he might have had with men. It was a subject we never discussed.

In 1953 while I was serving as an Assistant Attorney General of Kansas the program chairman of the Topeka Rotary Club asked me to speak about my experiences as a War Crimes Investigator in Korea. At a meeting with him I admired several abstract oil paintings on his office walls. He told me that they were his son's paintings. His son lived in New York City and he said we should meet some day. On one of the son's visits home we did meet, and we had immediate rapport.

A year or so later after leaving Topeka and joining the Southwestern Bell Telephone Company's legal department in Saint Louis, I had occasion to visit the artist while on a business trip to New York. He lived in Greenwich Village in a fantastic sky-loft above the Cherry Lane Theatre. The large windows of his studio looked out on a neighboring house once occupied by the poet Edna St. Vincent Millay. We talked of his work and I bought two paintings. Previously, the longest time I'd spent in New York City was in 1944 prior to departing on the troop ship Queen Mary for the war in Europe. And here I was in the heart of the Village – probably then the center of gay life in America. He was gay and it seemed only natural to engage in mutual masturbation.

These experiences with Brian and the artist were purely physical, with no feeling of love. They were in some way to my mind a simple extension of a handshake or a hug. Delightful and fulfilling, no threat whatsoever, I mistakenly then believed, to my happy marriage.

Over the thirty-one years of my career as a corporate lawyer with the Bell System it was necessary to take several bar exams as I was frequently promoted and moved from state to state—five altogether including my first admission in Kansas. Knowing how important it was not to fail, with each move I took a bar review course and lived for a week or more away from my family for concentrated study – the downtown YMCA in Saint Louis; the Stoneleigh Hotel in the Oak Lawn district of Dallas; the downtown YMCA in Portland, Oregon; and the Seattle Athletic Club in Washington. (Eventually promotions and moves took us to Cleveland, Ohio, and New York City where state reciprocity for experienced lawyers made bar exams unnecessary.) Just as being separated from my wife during war had done, these bar review absences set the scene for an occasional sexual encounter with another guy.

In Saint Louis there was a brief experience in the Y steam room. I later found that I was infected with pubic lice and honestly thought I had gotten crabs from a filthy toilet seat at the city's soon-to-be-abandoned airport. While awaiting a delayed flight to Dallas I had spent the better part of an hour reading the shocking graffiti scribbled everywhere on the stall walls. During World War II, the soldiers I knew who got crabs had had to shave their pubes and be soaked with iodine. When the horrible itching started in Dallas, I called my best man Bob Stewart, then a doctor, for an appointment. He briefly examined my shaved crotch, laughed at my ignorance in thinking it was necessary, and immediately prescribed A200, which did the trick.

To my embarrassment and shame I had by this time passed the pubic crabs on to my wife. Again A200 did the trick and only recently did Sari tell me that I was wrong in still believing I had contracted the varmint from a toilet seat.

When did she learn the truth about how pubic crabs are spread? Whenever it was, she must have realized that I had had physical contact with another person. That brief encounter in the YMCA steam room – and not the toilet seat – was the cause of my discomfort. And it took me more than fifty years to realize it.

Which brings me to a mind-boggling subject. When did my wife know, or even suspect, that I must be gay? And why didn't she face the matter sooner than that 1977 morning in New York when after intercourse she calmly said, "Your boys want to know if Richard is your lover."

While the two of us were reading my war year letters in the spring of 2004, she mentioned that in the early 1960s, when we were living in the Pacific Northwest, one of the telephone company wives had told her I was gay. This surprised me. She said she couldn't remember who it was and I can't imagine. Never in my career did I have sex with an employee or colleague in the several companies for which I worked.

Many years after retiring from the Bell System in 1985, I visited the two principal mentors in my life in order to ask them whether either had ever suspected that I was homosexual. The first was Walter W. Straley, first president of Pacific Northwest Bell Telephone Company. A spin-off from Pacific Telephone and Telegraph Company, Pacific Northwest Bell served the states of Oregon and Washington, and the northern part of Idaho. In 1961 Walt hired me as his vice president and general counsel, thereby making me the youngest lawyer in the Bell System with that level job. He was a brilliant writer as well as an outstanding leader in many Seattle cultural and civic endeavors. One essay, which he wrote for our company magazine, was entitled “It’s Okay to Play the Flute”. Having begun my own Bell System career in Saint Louis appearing as Harry Brock in The Kirkwood Theatre Guild’s production of Born Yesterday, I found the following excerpts from Walt’s essay particularly appropriate.

Some 25 years ago I appeared for a week of evenings and two matinees in a community theatre production of a play called ‘The Male Animal’. Cavorting and braying as the flamboyant football player, I won a prize for acting... During that week, morning bus rides toward the telephone company and my prosaic involvement at a low level of its affairs were made in a rosy glow from last night’s curtain calls... Shortly, the phone bade me to the boss’ office. ‘I hear you are in a play’, he said, and my antenna quivered with the effort to tune him in. ‘Yes sir’, I said, with my boyishself-deprecating-smile. ‘Well then’, he said, ‘I have some advice for you... if you want to go somewhere in this business... you got to make up your mind some place along the way just what you’re going to be, a telephone man or something else... an actor or a telephone man. You can’t be both’. For twenty-five years, I’ve been supplying a chain of brilliant and sometimes bawdy rejoinders to that pronouncement. At the time I didn’t say anything. Today’s response: I hope to turn out to be a little of each, and solely, neither... Somewhere out there in the beginning corporate world where I no longer dwell... is a young man who plays the flute and who hoped it would one day support him. Another wears his hair too long and has never owned a hat. That one thinks government should own telephone companies and has among his friends a girl who marched at Selma. There’s a girl with a passion for modern music and paintings made of rags and tags and cardboard boxes. For convenience, I speak of you as one. It’s O.K. to play the flute. Now... I must add quickly I’m not going to give you any time off for flute playing. Keeping your life in balance is your problem. But you can't, I say, be wholly alive if you give yourself wholly to our institution. We'll live longer with lively ones. So it's O.K. to play the flute. Of course, I've never been able to understand why you guys call yourselves flautists. And it is a kind of sissy instrument. (signed) W W Straley

Walter and his wife Rachel, for whom I cared a great deal, returned to Seattle from New York City following his retirement as AT&T Vice President Public Relations. Whenever I was on the West Coast I visited them and on this occasion in 1998 they consented to my taping our conversation. By then they knew of Sari's and my divorce and the reason for it.

We first reminisced about the original staff he had hired when President of the newly formed company, sadly realizing that I was the only one still living. Not wanting to pose immediately the "homosexual" question I had come to inquire about, I steered the conversation to some things I especially remembered about our times together in Seattle.

I asked him if he remembered the time he told us of one of his and Rachel's visits to Mona's, the famous drag bar in San Francisco. He laughed and immediately repeated the story of their group tour to North Beach. The drag queen sitting next to him at the bar was so convincing, he actually thought she was a woman.

"As a matter of fact I was so taken with him that I stayed on after the others had left," Walt said. "I leaned on the bar and he had on this exquisite perfume. He fanned his huge false eyelashes at me – and I found myself looking – down at his cleavage. Finally he grinned and let me know, in a very kindly but firm way, that (a) he was a man, and (b) I should stop thinking about what I was thinking because he wasn't interested."

As it turned out I didn't have to ask the "when did you first suspect" question. The following transcript of our taped conversation tells the story.

DEAN: I remember one time Charlie Ryan, General Attorney from AT&T's legal department came to Seattle. I had a little group together – John Rupp, Don MacLain, and my recent hire Dick Bromley, a brilliant young lawyer who with his wife had been U.S. figure skating champion – my staff in other words. I was hoping we'd have a nice lunch together and, as you may recall, Charlie Ryan had a bit of a drinking problem. He ordered a martini.
WALT: Huh...
D: When he reached out to the martini to get his glass, his hand was shaking so he couldn't hold the glass. He took this large, beautiful white linen napkin, put it around his neck, held the glass with one end of the napkin, pulled the other end with his left hand and he was able to steady that martini up to his lips and drink. I looked around and here's Dick Bromley, a Mormon who doesn't drink anything and I'm trying to impress my staff – he was a fairly new hire and I thought, "Good God.
What is Dick going to think of the legal department from New York. Do you remember me telling you about that?
W: Yes, I remember that.
D: One other time you did something that – we were having lunch at the Harbour Club. It was a beautiful day and I was looking out at the Smith Tower and I said, "I really love looking at that building and you looked at me and said, "Ostrum, I know why you like that, it's so phallic." Do you remember ever saying that to me?
W: Saying what?
D: Phallic
W: I don't.
D: Well, you've answered my question. You don't remember it. I thought afterward, I wonder if Walter's trying to tell me something about myself. Either I'm not aware of it or I am aware of it and he's just kidding me, but that's what you said to me.
W: At what age did you – uh, not only discover, but act upon the fact that you were – uh, gay?
D: A gay man?

W: Uh-huh.

D: Well, so far as first, you know, being attracted to guys, I suppose, very young.

W: Uh-huh.

D: Yeah, but I wouldn't have classified – we didn't have words for these things. In junior high, my first experience acting on it – junior high, high school there were several buddies, you know, and in college, too, but I always felt that everybody was probably like this. I never had any feeling that something's wrong with me, sickness –

W: Never?

D: None of that. I just – it was a part of me and I thought everybody did this and then they got married. After marriage the first time it happened in a way that I was aware of what my true sexuality was, then it bothered me. I wanted to tell Sari, but then I just didn't have the guts to do it, I guess, and so I resisted for years. All the time I was here in Portland and Seattle –

W: That's what I wanted to know.

D: No, I wasn't active with anyone then, but after I went to Cleveland I met someone I really enjoyed being with and it just went on from there, you know, and gradually we worked it out.

W: It doesn't strike me as being tragic at all.

D: No, it's not tragic at all. And I'm so happy that I have my wonderful children. In my church there are these young people – lesbian and gay – who want children so badly – they either adopt or one woman will have a child and it may be a little difficult to work out – society being what it is, but things have gotten better.

RACHEL: Oh, yes.

D: Things have gotten better. Even my mother – when my brother realized that I was probably going to separate from Sari – his wife said, "Okay, Dean, but don't ever tell your mother. It would kill her." [I then told them about the conversations with my mother that I wrote about in Chapter 3 above, ending with my mother saying "I just want you to be happy."]

W: (laughs)
R: Yeah.
D: And you never suspected that I might be gay?
R: No.
W: No.
D: Was it just because of children, and –
W: No, you were completely –
D: I'm not the stereotypical person that –
W: No, you weren't. You were happy or you always seemed to be a happy person –
D: Oh, I was.
W: You didn't go off at parties and sit looking out glumly at the group. There was no reason to –
D: I was satisfied with my life. I could have gone on forever. I would have gone ahead if we could have worked something out.
W: I think I was, I was surprised at – but very happy for you –
D: Thank you, Walter –
W: ...when someone told me about it.
D: Who told you? Or did I tell you?
W: I think you told me.
The other mentor in my life was Irwin L. "Jack" Luthi, my high school debate coach who also directed me in several plays. Just eleven years my senior, he was drafted following Pearl Harbor and stayed in service in the Regular Army, rising to full Colonel. He went on to a career as Provost of Washburn University in Topeka, and retired to Woodward, Oklahoma, where he served as City Manager and helped establish a lively community theatre. I visited Jack in 1998, the same year I spoke with Walter and Rachel Straley, (both of whom lived only a short time after my visit to Seattle). Our taped conversation follows.
JACK: I'm 87 years old but by the grace of God I still feel well. I've had a lot of repair jobs along the way, but so far they've been successful.

DEAN: Jack, let me ask you. This is getting into an area that I'm going to be thinking about and writing about, because I'm writing my memoirs now.
J: Yes.
D: And –
J: Which is great.
D: Which is great – but it's also sort of a challenge. If I'm going to be honest about my memoirs I have to deal with a subject that I'd like to talk a little bit about. It's my sexuality.
J: Hmm.
D: I've learned – I probably should have known when I was five years old – that I was gifted with being gay. And I do consider it a gift, believe me. I do. I think it's not something we choose. I know I didn't choose it. But when it finally evolved in my life – uh – it became a great relief to me – believe it or not – to be honest with my wife, my children, and my friends. It was escaping from what was really a double life.
J: Uh – huh.
D: I was very discrete in what was happening in my life – but I wasn't as discrete as I thought I was. My wife finally faced me with the – the fact that I was gay. And we discussed it – and worked it out finally – and we decided to separate. I've been with a dear friend for twenty-four years now – a guy, Richard. And so – I'm very happy. My family is very accepting, but since you meant so much to me in my life – you still do, I just – reflecting on this part of me that I have to write about – I would be very interested in knowing, did you ever – . Well, first of all, you've known gay people in your career, all of these five careers you've had, from time to time I'm sure – uh – did you ever suspect at all, that as I was growing up in high school, that I might be gay?
J: Never.
D: Never at all?
J: Not in my wildest imagination.
D: Oh?
J: I never – that thought never ever occurred to me.

D: Is it because – why do you suppose that is? Is it what you think a gay person should be like?
J: I really don't know – I really can't answer that, Dean, because I really don't know. Uh – it just never was a part of my life or part of my thinking process. And we had another young man in high school that, in the same category, you know.
D: Yeah.
J: He made a trip with me to – I won't mention the name because –
D: That's okay.
J: Made a trip with me to Europe, you know, went on a hell-of-a-trip and his parents were able to send him along – and he made that trip with me. Here again, I – it never occurred to me –
D: Never did –
J: But that – I say in those days – it wasn't that long ago – but that wasn't an issue that it is today. I mean people didn't even mention it.
D: You just didn't talk about it –
J: Didn't even talk about it I guess even if you knew it.
D: Right.
J: But, no, I would never – I would never have even – it never even occurred to me – never, never.
D: I hope it didn't make any difference in our –
J: No, absolutely no – I have now, I guess, educated myself in the years – that, you know, we're all human beings and we're all of the human race, but we're not all the same.
D: Oh, we're all different.
J: We're all different and this is one of the differences – a pretty fundamental difference, but it is a difference and it does not have any bearing whatsoever on my thinking toward that person, or my relationship with them, because I take them for what they are, and what they do, and what they've accomplished, and that's the important thing.
D: Right.
J: The other part is not important to me at all.

D: No, of course, it wouldn't be. Well, I wish more people were like you.

J: Well – I think, maybe, that will come.

D: Are you of the opinion, that as I've already expressed here, your sexuality is something you're born with, it's not acquired?

Or do you think it's something you choose?

J: No. I think you're born with it. Soon after my visit to Jack Luthi in Oklahoma I went back to my hometown to speak with a friend who was the sister of my father's longtime secretary. She was now a widow with three fine sons living elsewhere in the States. I asked her if after learning of Sari's and my divorce, and the reason for it, she had been surprised, or if she had ever before thought I might be gay.

"Why it was never even dreamed of," she insisted. "You were a married man with children."

Though I knew that one of her sons was gay and out, I resisted the temptation to discuss the subject further. I thanked her for her honest answer and left shortly thereafter.

Following the above three visits to learn if either of my two mentors or a longtime friend in my hometown had ever suspected me of being gay, I made a final visit to Belva Ostrum, the widow of my father's youngest brother Francis. She was then ninety-three years old, living in a nursing home in Hill City, Kansas, yet still alert and the vibrant, fun, outspoken person I had always remembered.

The purpose of this last visit was to record her telling me again of my uncle's reaction to the startling news of Sari"s and my 1980 divorce and my gayness. The tape of our conversation follows.

DEAN: Belva, tell me about when – this is very interesting –I want a record of it – hear it again from your mouth: When Sari and I got divorced or separated, the first time I came back to Hays, you were living in Hays, what did Uncle Francis, my uncle, Okas's brother, say to you about Dean?

BELVA: I don't know.
D: You don't remember that.
B: No.
D: Didn't he say, "Well, he's no different than he ever was – he's the same guy.
B: You came to see us.
D: Yes –
B: And between us we assumed – hey, look – I thought I'd never feel the same toward Dean again – and Sari. And then you came up to see us right away, and I said, "Well, Francis, Dean's the same old sweet thing!"
D: He's not a "meany"?
B: And he said, "Well, that's what I think."

Belva died in 2004, only a few months short of being one hundred years old. Both Richard and I remember her fondly. She had asked me how he was before I turned the tape recorder on that day and said she just wanted to be sure we were still together. Francis had been a bachelor until his late thirties when they married. He lived with my family for a time during the depression and when I was a little boy we shared a bed one winter. He was a Bethany College graduate and worked as a young man in a fine book store before being trained by my father to become a successful Abstracter of Titles in Hays, Kansas. His and Belva's ability to accept my gayness as a fact that didn't change their feeling toward me was something that truly warmed my heart.

Looking back on these three taped conversations it seems that my sexual orientation had no effect on how I came across to others. Had it been otherwise my many years in military service might not have happened.

But they did. And here follows the account of those military years.

Kindergarten teacher: Miss Leach

CHAPTER SEVEN: The Military Years

*D*ean Ostrum – a combat infantryman? You've got to be kidding.

In high school I wasn't even an athlete. My only time on the football field was at half time, as drum major of the band. At basketball games I conducted the pep band – from the sidelines. Though frequently elected a class officer, I was more often among the last chosen for activities involving a ball. Horseback riding and tennis were sports I loved. Boxing and gymnastics were sports I avoided. Since I was unable to swim, I rose no higher in scouting than second class. Being prone to motion sickness, carnival rides were anathema to my being. How on earth, then, did I ever become a rifle platoon leader, survive ten months of combat in World War II, not to mention an eleven-month recall as an army infantry captain in the Korean War? How did I survive being taken prisoner by the Germans during the Battle of the Bulge, and later escaping?

I think my ability to survive – without a scratch – was due to luck. Luck, luck, and more luck. Being at the right place at the right time. I never had pull to get safe assignments. I went where I was ordered and did what I was told – always with the hope of returning to my loved ones just as soon as possible.

In addition to luck, two other factors probably played a role. First, nature – the genes I inherited from my parents (tough, farming Swedish peasant stock on my father's side and loving, hardworking German stock on my mother's). Second, nurture – the times in which I grew up (mid-century rural America with her dust bowls, the Great Depression and all sorts of competitive activities in which I engaged – debate, drama, public speaking, music, and academics).

Like most small towns in America after World War I, Russell had an active, enthusiastic Post of the American Legion. It was a place for veterans to socialize, drink (despite prohibition), play cards, reminisce, and bond. My father-in-law Raymond Pierpont was a devoted Legionnaire in Chanute, Kansas, having seen combat as a machine gun squad leader in the trenches at Verdun. Louis Waldo (Wog) Banker, the father of two of my close friends and later Sigma Nu Fraternity brothers, was particularly active having served as enlisted representative of his 353rd Infantry Regiment at the Paris meeting to effect preliminary organization of the American Legion, following the Armistice. (Other of my friends' fathers who were Legionnaires were Doran Dole – Bob's dad, Ben Brooks, Ben Rein, & Ben Pflegar.)

Though my dad, Oscar Ostrum, had been a First Lieutenant in the Russell County Home Guard, he was never called to active duty and accordingly was not eligible to be a member of our local American Legion Post. (My family had little interest in things military; no one went hunting, and we didn't even own a gun. I do remember, however, that my maternal grandfather, Daniel Gross, owned a few shotguns – always securely locked in a case in my grandparents' home in Bunker Hill. My brother and I were often warned to leave them alone and never touch them.) After the Korean War in 1951 when I returned to Russell and ran for County Attorney, I joined the American Legion and Veterans of Foreign Wars for business and political contacts. Unlike today when lawyers advertise on television, in newspapers, and on subway cars, legal ethics then forbade any kind of advertising beyond having your name on your office door.

In the nineteen thirties the mood of our country was strictly isolationist. The Great War had been fought to end all wars and despite President Woodrow Wilson's efforts the United States had refused to join its Allies in the League of Nations. During my last years of high school we became keenly aware of the rise of Hitler and Mussolini, and of fascism generally. While there was no television we frequently listened to the frantic voice of Hitler ranting on the radio and saw newsreels at our local cinema.

On September l, 1939, when Hitler invaded Poland, I was just going into my senior year of high school. We followed the news as England and France issued ultimatums for his withdrawal by September 3rd and, when ignored, declared war. The Germans invaded Belgium the following May. The British barely escaped at Dunkirk, and France surrendered on June 21, 1940. A new word – blitzkrieg – came into our vocabulary, and the German "lightning war" soon changed my life.

In the fall of 1940 I left home for college. (I had chosen the University of Kansas rather than my father's and many of my uncles' alma mater – Bethany College in Lindsborg. Bethany was a small Swedish college known mostly for its excellence in music and art. It was also our band leader, Philip Boughner's school and I had often entered their spring woodwind music competitions winning second, third, and eventually first place with a small stipend toward tuition should I choose to go there. Boofie, as we called him, was a Legionnaire, played a mean trumpet, drove an impressive dark green Packard sedan purchased with his veteran's bonus, had a charming wife, and was greatly liked and respected. Had young, dashing Jack Luthi not come to our high school and steered me into speech, debate and drama, I might well have gone to Bethany, chosen instrumental music as a career and never graduated Yale Law School.)

At Lawrence, fraternities and sororities were big and the pressure to join was even bigger. Rushed mainly by the Banker family I and my best friend Victor Dolecek pledged Sigma Nu – a national fraternity known then on the Hill for lively parties, a few varsity athletes, several campus leaders, a charming housemother, average grades and not much else. I was actually spiked Sigma Nu (spiking was illegal) ahead of rush week and despite an interest in two other fraternities (the Phi Delts and the Betas) I kept my promise and chose Sigma Nu.

Victor and several of my frat brothers were later killed in action, but at the time, despite the news from Europe, war was not much on our minds. Even so it was in that freshman year of college that I took the first step leading to eventual military service. Two brothers – Nick Hoffman (later I dated his Kappa Kappa Gamma sister Jean) and Dan Hopkins (the Commander of our house and son of a respected Federal Judge who was also a Sigma Nu) – had top leadership roles in K.U.'s infantry Reserve Officer Training Corps (ROTC). Both Nick and Dan gave encouragement and several of us freshmen pledges (close friends Bob Fairchild, J.F. Kelsey, a few others and myself) enrolled in ROTC. We wore uniforms, paraded frequently, and studied military history and tactics. I also got to shoot my first gun, a 22 rifle, on the Corps indoor firing range.

Beginning in 1941 the war in Europe intensified. The Nazis occupied Norway and Denmark and the German Air Force began bombing London – all troubling events, but still far away. My sophomore year I studied hard, partied occasionally, dated several different girls, played in the University band, acted in a play, wrote biographical sketches for our annual (The Jayhawker) and a gossip column for the University's Daily Kansan. Life was carefree. My grades were mostly A's and to my parents' joy I was soon awarded a Summerfield Scholarship – the most coveted and valuable scholarship the University then had to offer. One Sunday morning in early December, however, everything changed. As a few of us late risers sat in the fraternity dining room eating breakfast, a brother rushed in, breathless.

"Japanese planes have bombed Pearl Harbor," he screamed.

We were soon at war. Orders from draft boards began arriving, and within a few weeks most of my fellow ROTC cadets and I had enlisted in the Army Reserve Corps. This allowed us to remain in college until expedited ROTC courses were completed. Since by going to summer school this would happen before we earned a college degree, no commission would be given – just a recommendation to

Officer Candidate School – presumably the Infantry School at Fort Benning, Georgia.

Fortunately for me I was able to remain in college long enough to meet my future wife Sari. We were engaged when I gave her a small diamond engagement ring in the spring of 1943, and married December 25 of that year, in Birmingham, Alabama. Following completion of all ROTC courses in the spring of 1943 I received orders to report to Tank Destroyer Officer Candidate School at Camp Hood (later Fort Hood), Texas. I had just completed my third year of college and been elected to Phi Beta Kappa, the honorary scholastic fraternity. Others of my class were sent to Artillery School, some to Tank School, and most to the Infantry School. Suddenly the principal weapon I was to be trained on was not an M-l rifle, but something much more powerful. The tank destroyer was a vehicle that looked like a Sherman tank except that its turret was open and its principle gun had a 3-inch barrel – much longer and larger than the Sherman 75-millimeter canon. Its effectiveness against the Desert Fox's (Rommel's) panzers had been proven beyond question in the decisive British victory at El Alamein in North Africa the previous year.

Active military service for this 128-pound, skinny, nonathletic, 21-year-old college kid – who barely looked eighteen – was about to begin.

OCS would be like boot camp, only tougher, and no one appreciated this more than one of my closest friends from high school, Johnny Hogue. I had worked summers for Johnny's parents' weekly newspaper, The Russell County News, as a reporter, proofreader, headline typesetter and all around flunky. He had taught me how to cover an American Legion baseball tournament and he was determined to get me in shape physically for the ordeal ahead. As a star high school athlete (later to be varsity catcher at Notre Dame University) he knew exactly what to do.

During the few weeks before I was to report to Tank Destroyer OCS, Johnny had me running daily on the high school track that circled our football field. Together we did all sorts of strenuous calisthenics and even played some softball catch. (One afternoon I took my eyes off the ball and got beaned so hard it knocked me backward onto the ground. For several days my forehead bore the stitch marks of that ball. Johnny later married one of my best drum majorettes from high school band days – the fun and lovely Laveeda Embree. Together they had six great kids, all boys. Johnny died way before his time, but I'll always love and remember him for the help he gave me, to make me fit.)

The physical demands of OCS were beyond what we'd imagined. Infiltration courses (crawling great distances under barbed wire with machine guns firing live ammunition overhead), rope climbing, wall climbing, push-ups, sit-ups, 25-mile marches under full field pack were our steady fare – all in a scorching hot, dry Texas summer with desert conditions and rattlesnakes aplenty. Being lean turned out to be an advantage as stocky, muscle-bound football types passed out in the heat. But I survived.

On September 16, 1943, I was commissioned a Second Lieutenant in the Tank Destroyer Corps, with army serial number O-529750. My fiancée, and my parents attended the graduation ceremony at Hood (and got to meet the wonderful mother- like woman, Mrs. Ater, who had befriended me and my buddy Lawson Jacks at the U.S.O. in Temple, Texas, the nearest town of any size to camp at Killeen). After a short leave I returned to Camp Hood to await assignment to a combat unit in the field. I really liked the striking-looking black and orange TD shoulder patch – the head of a ferocious tiger crunching a tank between its jaws – but I didn't get to wear it for long.

With the North African campaign successfully behind it, the army soon discovered that it had trained too many tank destroyer officers and most of my class were transferred back to the ROTC army branch from which we'd come. Four of us (Jim Newberry, Lefty Stavros, a pre-med student from West Virginia whose name I've forgotten, and I) were assigned to the 48th Armored Infantry Battalion of the Seventh Armored Division then stationed at Fort Benning. Our first night there saw us ripping off our hard-earned TD shoulder patches and quickly sewing on the red, white and blue patches of an armored division – a tank with a lightning bolt emblazoned on it, topped with the numeral 7.

My months in combat began the first night after debarking on Omaha Beach in August. The Seventh Armored Division lead the breakout at Saint Lô, Normandy, and spearheaded General Patton's Third Army drive across France. My friend and OSC classmate Jim Newberry was the first casualty in our entire division – shot through the head by a German sniper hours after debarking on Omaha Beach. Lefty Stavros died from severe wounds received on August 14 during our drive across France; and the classmate whose name escapes me was severely wounded and evacuated stateside at a later date.

Without a doubt the greatest piece of luck I had in military service was being made permanent Adjutant of the 48th Armored Infantry Battalion shortly after our arrival in England on June 14, 1944. Before that I was a rifle platoon leader in Company C (commanded by my close friend Harrison S. "Hassie" Forrester) and acting Adjutant only until our Division reached England. The Adjutant, First Lieutenant Andrews Allen, had gone to England as part of the Division advance party some weeks ahead of us. Since Andy could not rise above First Lieutenant as Adjutant he talked the Battalion Commander (then Major and later Lieutenant Colonel Richard D. Chappuis) into giving him a line assignment whereby he could eventually make Captain. A silver star, a couple of bronze stars, and several purple hearts later Andy did make Captain. He and Hassie luckily missed the Battle of the Bulge because of hospitalizations. I received a battlefield promotion to First Lieutenant on October 1. The next day, my wonderful platoon sergeant Grady H. Blazier, the acting leader of my former platoon, received a battlefield commission to Second Lieutenant. Proudly wearing his new gold bars he was picked off by a sniper that same night and died instantly.

Luck remained with me throughout our drive across France and our move to fight with the British Second Army in Holland. Though our battalion rear command post was often in range of German artillery, mortar, and "screaming meemie" Nebelwerfer shelling, it was a profoundly safer place than on the line. Many were wounded and a few killed around me, but I was spared.

And then came the Bulge.

The date was December 16, 1944. The days were short and the nights had been cold, damp, and overcast. The 7th Armored Division had earned a rest in Holland. As part of the British Second Army it had successfully repulsed German efforts to trap our parachutists at Arnhem (later popularized in the movie A Bridge Too Far). Rumor had it that as a part of the newly formed Ninth Army we would soon be part of a concentrated, all-out effort to cross the Rhine into Germany. At around ten o'clock that evening I was sent to Division headquarters and made a part of an advance party with orders to proceed immediately to St. Vith deep in the Ardennes forest of Belgium.

The little information given us was that our entire armored division was being moved to check a German thrust into a lightly defended and extremely broad front manned mostly by a very green 106th Infantry Division, a part of First Army to our south. Unlike our heavily armored tanks, motorized artillery, and infantry half-tracks, an advance party moves rapidly with jeeps carrying mostly personnel and supply officers. In this case we were to be lead by a few lightly armored vehicles from our 87th Reconnaissance Squadron. Our purpose in moving ahead of the main body was to select assembly points around Vielsam and to choose the best possible locations for various command posts in St. Vith.

That night our march south took us very close to the large city of Liège (in Belgium). For the first time I heard German buzz bombs, the bombs that had so terrorized London throughout the Blitz, screaming overhead and exploding in the environs of Liège. Moving rapidly, it wasn't long before we had covered about 100 kilometers and had come to the environs of St. Vith. There was still no word as to what exactly had happened, but it wasn't long before it was clear that the German thrust was not a minor matter. We later learned that two entire regiments of the 106th Infantry Division had been surrounded to our east. Many men and vehicles of supporting units were already fleeing to the rear in panic over what had happened. In many instances our tanks and infantry half-tracks would have great difficulty moving forward due to roads clogged by retreating Americans.

The news got grimmer still. Soon after daylight on the 17th there was a later-to-be-confirmed rumor of a German massacre of American prisoners at Malmedy, north and west of where we were. By the evening of December 17 the 48th Armored Infantry Battalion had closed on St. Vith and taken up defensive positions around its vital crossroads. But bad news continued to mount. Reliable reports confirmed the fact that German panzers had already made advances some forty miles to our rear.

When in combat, the Battalion Commanding Officer and his S-3 Operations Officer are usually located in the forward command post near the front lines. The Battalion Executive Officer (second in command), the S-1 Personnel Officer (Adjutant), the S-2 Intelligence Officer and the Battalion Aid Station are usually located somewhat to the rear. Always in the range of artillery and often mortar fire, the battalion's rear command post should be out of the range of small arms and machine gun fire. As Adjutant my job was to oversee all matters pertaining to personnel. That meant daily morning reports of each company's personnel status and especially the reception and assignment of officer and enlisted replacements for those wounded, killed or missing in action.

On the morning of December 18 things seemed calmer. The 48th Armored Infantry Battalion was in place around St. Vith, the 40th Tank Battalion had closed during the night and only our supporting artillery (hampered by traffic jamming the narrow roads) had yet to arrive. Curious to learn more about what was happening, I asked our Executive Officer (Major Lynn Carlson) if he minded me accompanying him and his driver on their morning visit to our forward command post. He made no objection so I climbed in the back of his jeep and we took off for St. Vith.

The narrow road wound through tall trees in the heavily wooded Ardennes forest. Just as we were rounding a sharp bend in the road, two German soldiers with submachine guns at the ready jumped in front of our jeep and screamed in German for us to halt. They were cleanly dressed in smart, well-tailored uniforms bearing, as I later observed, insignia of the elite SS Gross Deutschland Division.

As our driver braked the jeep to a sudden stop the German on our right rushed up to Major Carlson and the two began to struggle. At the same moment I quickly removed my 45-caliber revolver from its holster and slid a round into its chamber. Immediately looking up I saw three more German soldiers rushing toward us from the ditches. It being obvious that resistance was folly, I yelled to the Major to stop struggling. Luckily for me the front seat of the jeep had obscured my loaded weapon and I dropped it to the floor as they ordered us to dismount.

Now prisoners of the Germans, the three of us were quickly herded into the woods and our jeep was removed from the road in preparation for the next American vehicle that might be ambushed at the roadblock. (Years later I learned that our captors were a large combat patrol – about 400 soldiers – of the Füehrer-Begleit-Brigade commanded by Oberst Otto Remer and not the SS Gross Deutschland Division. That division was still on the Russian front, but soldiers from it had been added to Remer's Brigade for Hitler's *Wacht am Rhein* offensive – which resulted later in what we now call the Battle of the Bulge. Remer had previously commanded Hitler's headquarters guard and had come to the Führer's attention by his prompt action to protect him during the unsuccessful July 1944 Putsch on his life.)

Once off the road the Germans searched us and discarded our helmets. The soldier who searched me was wearing insignia of the SS Gross Deutschland Division and appeared unusually interested in the first aid pack he had removed from my web belt. He shook it gingerly and ultimately threw it as far as he could into the underbrush. Having up to that time served only on the Russian front, it is likely that he was unfamiliar with GI equipment and thought it some kind of grenade.

As soon as we had been shaken down we were herded farther into the woods. There we joined approximately fifteen other American officers and enlisted men who had been taken prisoner at the same roadblock. The only one I recognized was First Sergeant Ralph Hepfler from Company B of our battalion. We half smiled at each other, shaking our heads in disbelief about what had happened to us. These were clearly crack German troops – splendidly uniformed, highly disciplined, heavily armed, arrogant acting and supremely confident of accomplishing their mission. "So you thought you were going to win the war," I overheard one German jeer in perfect English.

The sudden realization that I was totally without freedom – a prisoner of the enemy and obliged to do whatever and go wherever my captors desired – was a psychological blow I find difficult to describe. I immediately envisioned my wife receiving a telegram saying I was missing in action. I could see my mother's face as she was given the dreadful news. I felt defeated and helpless.

Then I recalled General George C. Patton, addressing us at a Division assembly in England before we left for France. His coarse language had shocked even our toughest half-track drivers. He crudely encouraged us to "grind the bastard krauts under our tank tracks" and peppered his remarks with the same four-letter f-word so common in the army – a word we had never before heard from the lips of a General. Suddenly I remembered one important thing from his remarks. "If you're ever taken prisoner," he had bellowed, "I order you to escape." And as a bit of invaluable added advice he emphasized that escape attempts be made early on, while the enemy is still preoccupied in battle and certainly before you find yourself in a POW camp. It was good advice. I then and there resolved to obey his order should an opportunity present itself.

Shortly after being taken prisoner, as we were all standing at the edge of a clearing in the woods, I heard the sound of an American vehicle approaching from our left. At first I assumed it was just another that had been captured in their ambush.

At a distance of about half a football field a weapons carrier with its bed covered in canvas came into view. It stopped. The passenger beside the driver dismounted and began walking toward us. When he was about halfway there he dropped to the ground as the Germans opened fire with a barrage of submachine gun fire. Several soldiers began piling out from the back of the canvas cover and all including the driver were slaughtered before our eyes.

In the seconds it took for this to happen I fell to the ground and began quickly crawling on all fours, hoping to reach cover and escape into the woods. Unfortunately the firing stopped almost as soon as it had started. Before going far I felt the kick of a German boot on my own. Since an escaping prisoner is fair game for execution I waited for the shot. Perhaps he misinterpreted my unarmed departure as an attempt to avoid being hit in the firefight. On the other hand, my blonde hair, blue eyes and youthful Aryan countenance may have softened his heart a bit. As I looked up following the kick, he smiled and his finger gesture to return implied friendship, not hatred.

Early that afternoon we prisoners were grouped together and made to lie down in front of a heavy machine gun emplacement the Germans had dug in behind us. At this point the ranking officer among us, Lieutenant Colonel Mente, a West Pointer, asked to speak with the German Officer in command. Fearful that we prisoners might soon meet the fate of those Americans in the Malmedy Massacre days earlier, Mente demanded that we be taken to the rear, in keeping with the Geneva Rules of Warfare.

But to no avail – word eventually came back that we would be taken from the zone of combat only after they had completed their mission. (We later learned that their mission was to knock out a battery of the 275th Armored Artillery Battalion that had heroically remained in place following the surrender of the two 106th Infantry Regiments it had been supporting.)

We were without rations, but hunger was the least of our worries. Soon the woods all around us were being sprayed with heavy American machine gun fire from our tanks. (Weapons have a distinctive sound and this was certainly friendly fire.) As lead splintered the tree bark just inches above us, I couldn't help thinking of the infiltration courses we had trained with in the States. These gun barrels, however, had no blocks under them and their slightest depression could have wiped us all out. After what seemed like hours the strafing stopped.

As darkness approached the Germans began preparations to move out. One of their officers had to be carried and it was evident that others had sustained casualties in whatever combat mission they had undertaken. We had no idea what it had been or whether it had succeeded. There had been low clouds all day and the winter air was becoming bitter. Allied air superiority was of no advantage since the sky had not been clear since our departure from Holland. When it was pitch dark the Germans packed up their heavy machine gun and proceeded to rouse their prisoners. Made to stand, we were then placed in the middle of a long single column. Between every two prisoners was interspersed a German soldier. They clamped our hands on the belt of the man in front of us and proceeded to move forward through the dense woods. In the darkness I only knew that a fellow prisoner was holding my belt from behind and that I was holding the belt of a German soldier ahead.

At times we moved forward for some distance without stopping. Mostly, however, it was a halting advance. At one stop I let go of the German belt I was holding and dropped to the ground. Several other prisoners apparently did likewise and the Germans immediately began screaming for us to rise. Instead of obeying I quickly crawled under the low branches of a large fir beside me. Undoubtedly the prisoner behind me – whoever he was – obeyed the command and reattached himself to my German because in the confusion I was not missed.

Suddenly I realized I was not alone. The warm body of another prisoner, a private, was pressing up beside me. I'll never forget his whispered words.

"Can I go with you, Lieutenant?" he asked.

I whispered back words to the effect that he was welcome, but I had no idea where it might be.

Though this frightened young soldier had been with us all day, I knew neither his name nor the outfit to which he belonged. (Officer prisoners had been kept separate. Communication between us had been minimal, though I had managed to speak to the saddened 2d Lieutenant who had dropped to the ground that morning as the Germans opened fire on his weapons carrier. He told me he had been lost, was looking for directions, and mistakenly thought all of us at the woods edge were Americans – that is until he got close enough to see who had weapons.)

After what seemed like a lifetime, the German column finally moved forward again. Curled up against each other, almost afraid to breathe, we were close enough to touch their heavy boots. We remained in place and still as mice as they moved away. I was about to speak when a German soldier came running back. Stopping directly beside us he called out loudly, "Fritz!" then "Heinz!" He apparently was missing two of his buddies. After each name he paused and listened. Then he called for them again. Finally, hearing no response he quickly turned and ran off to catch up with the departing German column.

So there we two were, alone in the forest, no longer prisoners, but completely in the dark – literally and figuratively – as to how to rejoin friendly forces. My companion was willing to follow my lead and I was very happy for his company. We had no map, no compass, no moon, nor stars to guide us. My sense of direction had never been good, but instinct told me that we should first find a road. To be inconspicuous we carefully darkened our faces and hands with damp soil from the ground. This accomplished, we moved out from our blessed fir tree and set out in search of a road.

Eventually we found one and proceeded to follow it until we reached a farmyard. As we approached the farmhouse we could hear the hushed voices of men and women speaking a foreign language. If the language had been French they might have been friendly, but since it sounded guttural like German, I decided we should take no chances, and we slipped away.

Following the road further we came to what looked like a small village. Several buildings were aflame and we could hear sounds of a battle coming from somewhere in the distance. Having no idea where we might be, I advanced to the first building still standing. Moving cautiously along its wall I reached the corner and slowly looked around it. To my horror I saw a German soldier, armed with a submachine gun, wearing that distinctive helmet, and peering in the opposite direction. He appeared to be on sentry duty and was gazing toward the burning town.

In what seemed like another lifetime I pulled back around the corner and we retreated again to the relative safety of our road. We now knew that the Germans might be anywhere and that re-capture was a distinct possibility.

What to do?

In the far distance I heard what to my ear was friendly artillery firing. In an Armored Division there are three Combat Commands – CCA, CCB and CCR. Each is comprised of an Armored Infantry Battalion, a Tank Battalion, and a mechanized Artillery Battalion. The sounds I was hearing were those of a 105-millimeter howitzer. Our objective was now clear. Our task would be to advance, somehow, toward that artillery fire and thereby return to friendly arms.

Exactly how we got there I don't remember. I know we eventually found ourselves in the cover of a ditch. Within voice range of this artillery battery, I hollered as loudly as I could to gain the gun crew's attention. We remained in the cover of the ditch telling them that we were escaped American prisoners and not Germans carrying hand grenades.

They finally gave us permission to come forward. And after we managed to convince them we were telling the truth, they welcomed us with open arms. Though not part of my 7th Armored Division they were all members of the 275th Armored Artillery Battalion that had been in support of the 106th Infantry Division when the German offensive began on December 16th. They told us how that very afternoon they had turned their guns and thrown grenades at an attacking German task force (our former captors, we now realized) and they proudly showed us dozens of hand grenade pin rings on their still gloved fingers.

We were immediately taken to their Battalion Commander, questioned about what had happened to us, given food (our first since before our capture) and bedded down in sleeping bags for a much-needed rest. We were two exhausted soldiers.

That night it began to snow and when we awakened the next morning the weather had turned even colder. I asked how I might be returned to my infantry battalion and was told to await a messenger who would take me to St.Vith. (To this day I can't remember the name of the enlisted man I escaped with – or even his unit if he ever told me. Should he still be living and ever read this account of our time together I hope he'll get in touch. In the meantime I remain grateful for his loyal company and thankful for our safe return to friendly troops.)

Later that morning a messenger took me by jeep to the CCR command post in St. Vith. "Where's your helmet, Lieutenant?" The Brigadier General barked at me. I hadn't expected to be hugged for escaping from the Germans, but would have welcomed a "Well done."

Much later in the day I was able to rejoin my battalion and "utter chaos" would be a good description of the events that followed my return. The situation got progressively worse – our ranks were being decimated. Germans were attacking with increasing strength in their efforts to drive us from our St. Vith Salient. The extent of our plight was made clear in the message we later learned had been sent to Corps Headquarters by our Commanding General, General Hasbrouck: "If we don't withdraw soon there'll no longer be a 7th Armored Division."

Thankfully his plea for relief was respected and we were eventually ordered to pull back. Later Field Marshall Montgomery wrote of our stand at St. Vith, "They can come back with all honor. They come back to more secure positions. They put up a wonderful show."

Our withdrawal was made in daylight with German tanks fast closing on our rear. Exhausted and depleted in men, ammunition and equipment, we had scarcely passed through friendly troops of the 82nd Airborne Division when orders came for an immediate counter-attack against a German force that had entered the nearby town of Manhay. By Christmas Eve this mission was accomplished.

At last we were given a brief respite from battle. Replacement officers and men joined us; lost equipment was replaced, and we then spent the last half of January in a new offensive to retake St. Vith. Fighting was ferocious, but the Germans eventually retreated to their original positions behind their West Wall.

January 1945 had been the severest winter the Ardennes had experienced in over forty years. Battle casualties on both sides during the Battle of the Bulge were staggering and frostbite took a tremendous further toll. I personally can't remember ever being so cold and miserable. But again, I survived.

Being a prisoner, even for a day, was the most helpless, hopeless feeling I've ever had. How brave Americans endured months and even years of captivity during World War II in Europe and Japan is hard to comprehend. I have known several men who were POWs, from my hometown – Dean Chase Banker in Germany and Ray Beck following the death march in Bataan. They have my never-ending sympathy and respect.

Back to the night of my escape, the withdrawing German column later encountered heavy machine gun fire from tanks of our 40th Tank Battalion as they passed through the woods. Several other prisoners were then able to escape, including my unharmed jeep mate Major Carlson, and Lieutenant Colonel Mente, severely wounded but alive. First Sergeant Ralph Hepfler of B Company did not escape that night, but was later liberated before ending up in a prisoner of war camp.

Sixteen years later I had just finished a business lunch at the Washington Athletic Club in Seattle and dropped by the men's room before returning to my office. Standing at the urinal I looked up as someone next to me suddenly said, "You're Dean Ostrum!" It was Ralph Hepfler.

By then I was Vice President and General Counsel of Pacific Northwest Bell Telephone Company and Ralph was the Chief Purser for Northwest Orient Airlines, flying frequent trips to Tokyo. Needless to say we retired to the club lounge and spent the remainder of the afternoon exchanging memories of the war. I was particularly interested in learning of the treatment he had received before liberation. It had been an extremely unpleasant experience for him – and one that might also have been mine had I not escaped.

In the fall of 1950 I was recalled to active duty for service in the Korean War, (at that time euphemistically called the Korean Conflict or the United Nations Police Action in Korea). When I said goodbye to my wife Sari and my daughter Karna in Seattle I truly thought I might not return. Then a Captain in the Army Reserve Corps, it was highly likely that I would again be assigned to a combat infantry unit upon arrival.

Once in Korea and standing in line to receive my unit assignment, my heart fell. I was hearing names of all those infantry divisions that had been hit the hardest after the Chinese joined the North Koreans and swept down from the Yalu River following the Chosen Reservoir debacle – "First Cavalry" – "2d Infantry" – and so on. But to my great surprise and relief I was assigned to Army War Crimes, investigating war atrocities and based in peaceful Pusan. Somehow my Yale Law School degree had saved me. My MOS (Military Occupational Specialty) included "lawyer" as well as "combat infantry officer."

Following return to the States in January 1952, and after the birth of our third child of four, I resigned my reserve officer commission. Recently I had occasion to look up my Certificate of Honorable Discharge. You see, I've prepaid my funeral expenses and the funeral home required a copy of this certificate if I'm to have an American flag on my casket. As a gay man this is important to me. No one ever asked and I certainly never told.

Looking at that certificate dated 16 September 1958 and made out to Dean G. Ostrum, Capt. Inf. USAR, I felt a bit of pride to read again the following words. "This certificate is awarded as a testimonial of Honest and Faithful Service to his country."

Sari and Dean's only wedding photo
1943 Columbus, Ohio

Our first car, a Buick Roadmaster

Dean's Harley bike in Heidelberg, Germany

CHAPTER EIGHT: Years After WWII

After returning from Europe following WWII, I resumed my college studies at the University of Kansas in Lawrence. Although it was now 1946 and I had spent only a short time living with my wife since our marriage on Christmas Day 1943, it was wonderful to be with her again.

Our second home – the first being in Columbus, Georgia – was a second floor studio apartment right above Don and Vivian Pierce. Don had played varsity football for KU and was then Director of Publicity for the University's Athletic Department. He was a walking encyclopedia of baseball statistics and often shared his knowledge with my wife who, like her father, was a great baseball fan. (Sari was also a fine swimmer and taught all of our children how to swim, a skill I never learned despite repeated attempts.)

As a returning service man, I was two or three years older than most of my classmates. There were quite a few of us service men. We tended to wear clothing purchased at surplus Army & Navy stores, and many of us were married, some with wives who were employed. Sari had taught band and orchestra in the Lawrence public schools while I was in Europe and she now got a job at the University Registrar's office.

Spring was the time the University of Kansas Annual, The Jayhawker, chose its editor for the coming school year. Since I had written many articles for annuals during my earlier years at KU, even taking several journalism courses and writing a gossip column for The University Daily Kansan, I was a natural to be considered for the editor's job. It also didn't hurt that my best man and fraternity brother Bob Stewart was dating Hannah Hedrick, a Kappa Kappa Gamma, who was the retiring editor. I was also a close friend of two earlier editors – John Conard and Mary Morrell (also a

Kappa). (John and I were both Summerfield Scholars. Geared to need, the scholarship would if necessary pay for one's entire college degree. It was awarded based on exams taken during senior year in high school, and granted at the end of freshman year in college, to a few students with high academic records. Though I had not succeeded the first time, my 4.0 (all A's) freshman year grade average caught their attention. In a letter replying to the notice of my selection my father wrote back words to the effect that while my parents didn't need monetary aid they were most appreciative of this honor. Being a Summerfield Scholar required that your grade point average remain high or you were put on probation. This happened to me in the fall semester after Sari and I were pinned. She found it disappointing that we had fewer dates during the spring semester while I studied extra hard to restore my grade point average to the level where I was no longer on probation. Though I was receiving no aid at the time it was important insurance for finishing college should financial need arise.)

Editing the 1947 Jayhawker was a highlight of my last year in college. Unlike most college annuals, which come out at the end of the school year, ours was published in four issues – eventually bound together in a handsome hardcover binder. The Fall issue had an early deadline and was followed by Christmas, Winter and Spring. Patterned in many ways after the then new LIFE Magazine, each of our issues was loaded with photos and contained articles and biographical sketches on student leaders and accomplished faculty.

The Jayhawker had an outstanding business manager, Dick Carmean, and this freed me to plan the content of each issue with the help of fine writers and a photo staff headed by the gifted Hank Brown. We featured many student activities and I especially enjoyed giving non-fraternity and black students recognition. Lunch-counter sit-ins by students protesting racial segregation in Lawrence were just beginning.

In the spring of 1947, with encouragement from my political science professor Hilden Gibson I applied for a

Rhodes Scholarship. None had been granted during the WWII years and competition was intense. It was also the first year a married student could apply.

The way it worked, you first had to be chosen to represent your University and next to represent your state. My memory is hazy as to the interviews, with the exception of the one I had with a former Kansas Governor and later unsuccessful Republican candidate for President of the United States – Alfred M. Landon. He was exceedingly warm and friendly. I was greatly impressed. As it turned out I was one of two chosen to represent Kansas at the regional final in Des Moines, Iowa.

The successful winner of a Rhodes Scholarship that year in Des Moines was a single young man who had graduated from West Point Military Academy and later earned a Master's degree. It was a disappointment for me, but not the end of the world. (Had I been successful in winning that scholarship I think I might have chosen a career in teaching.)

So what to do next? Since my high school debate coach and mentor Jack Luthi had steered me away from a possible career in public school music, and my father had always been an outstanding example of a man who cared deeply for others and served with great honor as a country lawyer, I decided to apply for law school.

Where to apply? I chose three schools – Michigan, Harvard, and Yale. First came a letter admitting me to Michigan. Before hearing from Harvard I was notified of my acceptance at Yale. My dad had helped his brother Carl Ostrum attend Yale Graduate School, so I felt a tie I couldn't resist. I chose Yale and notified Michigan and Harvard of my decision – a choice I never regretted and to this day am grateful to have made.

Yale was a perfect place for me in innumerable ways. While I missed making the Yale Law Journal, I did finish in the top 20% of my class, served on the boards of the Yale Moot Court and the Barristers Union, and received two top prizes with classmate Arthur Littleworth.

Our first year in New Haven we shared a small, two-story frame beach house with Ferd and Donna Evans in Milford, Connecticut, near the shore on Long Island Sound. Ferd was doing graduate work at the law school and came from Wichita, Kansas. My classmate Charles Baron and his wife Betty from Saint Louis lived in a nearby beach house in Milford. Sari and Betty were both pregnant and often took walks together on the beach. Because of the half hour commute to the campus, we older married students only saw our unmarried, mostly younger classmates during class hours.

Karna was born in Grace New Haven Hospital on April 13, 1948, the spring of that first year in New Haven. She was a couple of weeks later than the due date the doctor had calculated. Sari's mother had come east to help and ended up spending two weeks with us before the baby was born. In those days there was no way of determining a baby's sex before birth. Fathers were kept from the delivery room and it was always a delightful surprise to learn the baby's sex and be told it was healthy with ten toes, ten fingers, and hearty lungs.

From the moment the nurse brought Karna wrapped in a blanket to the room where I was waiting I knew she would be special. Unlike most newborns (and as it turned out, unlike our three boys), Karna held her head up all by herself and looked around with wide-open little blue eyes, curious to see the world around her. Eventually she had blonde hair with curls, but in her first year she looked more like a cute little boy.

After Grandma Marjorie returned to Kansas it was occasionally necessary for me to take the middle-of-the-night feeding. I'll never forget the night during spring semester final exams when the baby awoke around 2 for her bottle. Our bedroom was on the second floor next to Ferd and Donna's (a paper-thin wall between us permitting little privacy for lovemaking – but that's another story). My objective was to give the baby her bottle as quickly as possible and get her back to sleep, thereby not disturbing Sari and our housemates from their slumber; and most important of all allowing me to return to bed for a few hours rest before heading into New Haven for a tough exam I'd been studying for.

Everything seemed to be working perfectly. The baby eagerly sucked on her bottle as I sat on the top step of the narrow stairs that led down to the small living room below. Inexperienced as I was it never occurred to me that a baby should be burped during her feeding and not just afterward. Accordingly, to my delight the entire bottle was consumed in record time and I took her up for the needed burp before we could both return to bed.

And the burp did come – a terrific one, followed quickly with the entire contents of a full bottle of formula. My shoulder was saturated as well as the entire length of stairs to the floor below. And dear Karna, her stomach empty, immediately began crying loudly – hungry again for her middle-of-the-night feeding.

By now, all are wide-awake – Sari, the Evanses, the baby, and her brand-new father. It was then that for a second I understood how parents must restrain themselves from an angry response to a disobedient child. I was the one at fault and my next half hour was spent cleaning up the staircase while Sari prepared a new bottle and fed the baby. Finally we all returned to our beds.

Although as a WWII veteran I was blessed with the G.I. Bill of Rights that paid for the Yale Law School tuition, it was still necessary to have money on which to live. Fortunately my dad, Oscar Ostrum, had an abstract business and needed typists to copy the endless pages that went into the thick Abstracts of Title that buyers received when they purchased real estate. Sari and I were good typists and my dad paid us by the page for the work we did.

That first summer away from New Haven, we returned to Chanute, Kansas, where Sari's parents lived and managed one of the several Calvert Clothing Stores that were the mainstay of Sari's mother's family business (started by Sari's grandfather). Sari's dad, Raymond Pierpont, had the necessary contact with the Chanute city fathers and I was given a job as a construction worker on an addition to the city power plant. My job was that of a simple laborer on a crew pushing wheelbarrows of cement and digging footings for foundations. It was backbreaking work and every night I was exhausted, finding sore muscles in body parts completely unused in going to law school. My co-workers somehow put up with me. Many spoke little English and probably wondered how I ever got the job.

Every day I took a sandwich and thermos and, having little in common with my fellow laborers, spent the lunch hour on the steps of the Episcopal Church rectory across the street from our construction site. The rector – whose name I no longer remember – was British, handsome, and quite young, perhaps in his early thirties. We became friends and because I wanted Karna to be baptized we arranged for him to perform the sacrament. Sari and her mother, being devout, and I really mean devout, Christian Scientists didn't believe in baptism, but cheerfully went along with my wishes. Grandpa Raymond who never attended their church, or any other for that matter, seemed happy to go along with the ceremony. Accordingly little Karna was baptized one summer evening with her parents and maternal grandparents in attendance. Incidentally the young priest had a fine collection of antique crystal and silver, some of which Sari's mother was able to purchase years later when he returned to England.

Fortunately for my sore back, an event occurred the following week that gave me the excuse to leave construction, depart Chanute, and take my wife and child to my parents' home in Russell. The event was my maternal grandmother Dango's fall, which broke her hip. My mother was completely devoted to her care and I wanted to be nearby, to help. Dango had made her home with my family since the day after my grandfather's death in 1936. (She eventually died at 91, blind and frail, sitting in her rocker in the bedroom of my parents' home.)

For the remainder of the summer I worked as a typist for Ben Brooks, a close family friend who was the County Register of Deeds. When Sari, Karna and I returned to New

Haven for my second year in law school we were able to rent a one-bedroom apartment in a new building in New Haven owned by the father of one of my classmates, Stan Jacobs. Privacy, at last.

It was here that we became close lifelong friends with my classmate Milt Mapes, a graduate of the U.S. Naval Academy and married to Sandra Clark, the niece of a prominent New Haven Federal Judge, Charles Clark. Milt loved children, but at that time had none of his own, and he became Uncle Milty to ours. (He and Sandra later divorced and he eventually married another of our classmates, Jane Richardson, a brilliant student whose family were Quakers. I had the honor of being Milt's best man at their wedding, in Denver, Colorado. Jane and Milt had three children, and Jane has remained a dear friend with whom Richard and I are in close touch to this very day. Sadly, Milt died far too young, of leukemia.)

At the beginning of our third year in New Haven we finally qualified for married student housing in one-half of a Quonset hut near the Yale Bowl and adjacent to the practice football field. Sari was then pregnant with our second child, John Pierpont Ostrum, who was born January 11, 1950. Again I was kept out of the delivery room and we were never asked if we wished our boy to be circumcised. In those days, and even later with our other two boys, it was the customary thing to do. (In 1997 when my youngest grandson Leif was born his father, my son Peter, inquired as to my thoughts on circumcision. We agreed that it was unnecessary and in retrospect I wish all my boys, like their father and my father before me, had never been circumcised.)

During my last year of law school my classmate Charles Baron and I got jobs as bartenders at the New Haven Lawn Club. We worked weekend nights for Yale functions, weddings, and one particularly memorable graduation party for young women from the Yale School of Nursing. One young woman, I remember, apparently ordering her first drink ever, insisted on Scotch with ginger ale. Yuck! For affairs like the Yale swimming team party, where Bob

Kipputh, the U.S. Olympic swim team coach attended, we served only straight-up martinis and Manhattans. These were powerful drinks since in those days we prepared them in gallon jugs and placed them in the freezers overnight. It would have been a sacrilege to allow an ice cube to touch a properly prepared Manhattan or martini.

Perhaps this would be a good time to recall what was going on insofar as the gay side of my life was concerned. And the answer is, nothing. After my wedding (December 25, 1943), and until I finished college and law school and began the practice of law with my father in Russell in the summer of 1950, there had been only the one experience in Germany after the end of the war. While my attraction to those of my own sex was strong, it was only in that hotel for transient officers in Augsburg, when the General's aide performed oral sex on me, that I realized how overpowering it could be given the right circumstances. And the right circumstances were always to allow the other guy to be the aggressor. No one likes rejection, but more importantly, I was fearful of being caught in an act that was then illegal and could ruin my military career as well. During all those years my attraction to young men like myself was present, but I resisted going forward with it. For example, the Yale Library men's room just across from the Law School seemed to be a hotbed of homosexual activity. The few times I was approached there I pretended disinterest.

My decision to return to Kansas and a small town law practice with my father was one that I fell into without much reflection. Had I made the Yale Law Journal I might have been inclined to try for a court clerkship or a job with a prominent big city law firm. I knew my father would like me to become his partner and I was grateful to him for having made it possible for me to marry young and complete both college and graduate school without financial worries. Also I have always loved people and the long hours of research in the law library of a big firm did not appeal to me.

My father picked out a small house at 663 East Sixth Street in Russell and gave it to us when we returned from

New Haven in the spring of 1950. It was our first of what turned out to be ten homes. The signs on his law office windows above the Russell County Building and Loan Association were changed from "Oscar Ostrum, Lawyer" to "Ostrum & Ostrum, Lawyers," the suite was redecorated with nicer furnishings, including valuable wood prints by a noted local artist Hubert Deines, and my practice of law began.

To supplement my income as Dad's partner I joined the local Army Reserve unit. The unit met weekly and would later that summer go for two weeks' training at Camp McCoy, Wisconsin. Most of my work in those early months was for long-time clients of my father. The only client who came to me solely on my own was Arlen Spector's brother-in-law. Like myself Arlen was a graduate of Russell High School and Yale Law School. He is now a United States Senator from Pennsylvania and chairman of the Senate Judiciary Committee. At that time his brother-in-law owned the local junkyard and needed a simple contract drawn. My time was mainly spent in closing estates for existing clients and it is likely that my family would barely have scraped by had I been on my own to earn a living practicing law in Russell, Kansas.

Here I must tell of something that happened that first summer that foretold the struggle I would later face, in spades, with my sexuality.

One of Dad's clients was a family whose daughter had come to us seeking a divorce. She and her young husband already had one child and she was pregnant with a second. About my age he had been a Marine with many months of combat service in the Pacific during World War II and was now employed as a truck driver for an oilfield supply company. My job was to talk to the young mother and see what I could do to save their marriage.

In our discussions the young woman told me that the sole reason she wanted a divorce was that her husband insisted on being nude in the privacy of their home, even in the presence of their young daughter. She agreed that I could talk with him and, if possible, work out some compromise. I believe that her religion (probably Catholic) had taught her that nudity was in some way shameful.

I arranged to meet with her husband one evening after work in an attempt to see what might be done. Since he and I were young war veterans and had both seen lots of combat, I bought a six-pack of beer and picked him up at their home for a drive out into the countryside where we could talk in private.

It was a warm summer night and we found a side road and parked. He told me that during his time in the Pacific theater, while not in combat, the Marines often sunned and swam nude and that he had developed a keen interest in visiting a nudist colony with his wife and child after returning to civilian life. He saw nothing wrong with being naked with his family in their home and I wholeheartedly agreed with him. As I've already stated in these memoirs, in my own home, growing up, nudity was not flaunted, but it was never a subject of shame. I occasionally saw my mother naked while she was bathing, and I remember my father doing nude calisthenics every morning in front of the mirror in their bedroom – just as in gyms today it is customary to watch yourself in a mirror as you lift free weights. (Incidentally I never saw my father with an erection, but I do recall that he seemed amply endowed as I observed his genitals while he was doing leg squats before the bedroom mirror.)

In short, the Marine and I – both combat infantrymen – felt that that I should talk with his wife again. He agreed that he would be willing to wear shorts when around his child at home on the condition that his wife would agree to spend their summer vacation at a nudist colony in the Ozarks and not complain about full family nudity on such occasions. He seemed relieved to reach this kind of compromise and I was hopeful it would save a marriage that seemed in every way worth saving.

About this time it was completely dark except for a full moon. The six-pack was almost finished and we both felt the need to take a leak, as he called it. Standing beside each other urinating on the side of the road was a completely natural thing for two young soldiers. On long training marches we had both participated in pee breaks with dozens of other men, lined up along a roadside ditch – all in full view of each other's privates (no pun intended).

On this evening it was a little different. We found each other attractive, and partial erections became obvious as the streams of urine took their upward paths.

When we returned to the front seat of the car the conversation turned to various sexual experiences we had had. I didn't resist when his hand found its way to my crotch. Both of us were hard by this time and we proceeded to lower our pants and shorts and engage in mutual masturbation. Eventually he leaned over and took me in his mouth – the second guy in my life to give me a most welcome blow-job.

I firmly believe that he was straight, but that sex with other men had not been unknown to him while he was in the service. When men are isolated from the society of women in wartime, as often happened in the south Pacific and during weeks and months aboard ship, there is little opportunity for heterosexual release. While I was not inclined that night to reciprocate orally I certainly did not hesitate to relieve him with my hand. And I felt there was nothing in any way wrong in what we had just done. Somehow I rationalized that if it was wrong, our attraction for each other was just another casualty of war – though one for which no purple hearts are given.

The next day I told my father about the compromise we had reached regarding nudity and we both expressed hope that this marriage would be saved. Only once thereafter did I see the Marine again. It was at a carnival at the county fairgrounds one evening a few weeks later. I was with my wife and two children. He was with several guys who looked like oilfield roustabouts. Our eyes met for a second, but that was all. A year or so later while on active duty in Korea I received a letter from my dad that mentioned that our client and her husband had divorced. The compromise had proved unsuccessful. What path my Marine's life eventually took I'll never know.

That same summer one of my dad's clients, a near destitute farmer with a wife and several children, was charged with the crime of cattle rustling (illegal branding of cattle) which in Kansas was a felony, punishable with time in prison. The prosecuting witness was a wealthy neighbor who was prominent in the Republican Party. The County Attorney Johnny Woelk, also a Republican and a high school friend of mine, had obtained a written confession from our client, and conviction appeared a certainty. The case was scheduled for early fall trial and Dad asked me to investigate the matter thoroughly in preparation. Underdogs have always had special appeal to me, so I welcomed the chance to do whatever could be done to keep this poor man out of prison. I visited his dilapidated farm and learned that it was the retarded brother of our client who had branded the one calf in question and not the accused himself. I also learned that it is not uncommon for a stray calf to join up with another herd of cattle should it be separated from its own – via a broken fence or whatever.

In the meantime I had returned from my Army Reserve unit's two-week training camp in Wisconsin, the Korean War had begun, and I was under orders to return to active duty with Fifth Army Headquarters in Chicago.

The illegal branding case came to trial only days before my scheduled departure. The jury had been impaneled, each side had made their opening statements, and the prosecution had rested after what appeared to be an open and shut case. The wealthy owner of the calf testified; over the objection of my father, the confession was received in evidence; and the Kansas state brand inspector, a somewhat effeminate man grandly dressed in boots, jodhpur riding breeches, and an Army-like Eisenhower jacket made from material called pinks, concluded their case.

Our defense was a simple one. Yes, the branding had occurred, but it was only an accident. The necessary criminal intent was absent.

My first witness was our client's retarded brother. Following the oath administered by the bailiff, he shyly took his seat and looked innocently around the courtroom. My first utterance was the routine request: "Please, state your name." He hesitated a moment before uttering just one word – his first name, Bob. Though we had never rehearsed this response, his manner and tone told the jury in no uncertain terms that this witness was more than a bit slow of wit. I gently asked him to give his full name and after a second "Bob" he understood what I meant and remembered to add his family name as well.

We then established that on the day in question he had done the branding himself, the accused was not present, and that there had been no intent whatsoever to rustle the rich neighbor's herd. We rested our defense; closing arguments were made; the judge instructed the jury and they retired to consider their verdict.

Following lunch we were called to the courthouse. Judge Spencer asked the foreman, "Have you reached a verdict?" "We have, your honor," the foreman responded. "We find the defendant NOT GUILTY."

Our client's wife broke down in sobs of relief.

My dad was proud, I could tell. It turned out to be the one and only criminal case we would ever try together. We helped bring about a result that was just. While we would never receive monetary payment for our efforts, the occasional steak from our client's butchering was compensation enough.

One hour after the verdict was announced, I boarded a Union Pacific train at our little depot and was on my way to Chicago. Once again, I was an active duty infantry officer, reporting for the second time in my life for a war.

By the fall of 1950, though wearing Captain's bars, the highly respected Combat Infantryman Badge, a Bronze Star, and many World War II combat ribbons, I was in no way prepared to lead an infantry company in combat. Fortunately my first active duty assignment was with the Fifth Army Headquarters in Chicago. Having a law degree I was designated a contracting officer and assigned the job of selecting the advertising agency that would design Fifth

Army's recruiting publicity in the several Midwestern states in its territory. The successful agency would receive no pay, but there was prestige in being selected on a public service basis. Accordingly many fine Chicago-based agencies made elaborate presentations.

My duties involved traveling to all five state recruiting main stations, and for the first month before my family could join me I lived in the bachelor officer quarters located in the Hyde Park area at Army Headquarters on Lake Michigan.

One evening I decided to go into the Loop (downtown Chicago) and attend a concert of the renowned Chicago Symphony Orchestra. While waiting for the train on the elevated Illinois Central (IC) platform I couldn't help noticing the graffiti scribbled on the station walls. For the first time in my life I saw the numerals "69" written in many places, and wondered what it stood for. A young man about my age spoke to me and we discovered coincidentally that we both had tickets that night for the same concert. He was a Navy veteran of World War II and gave me his phone number with the suggestion that we get together one evening for dinner at his apartment near Army Headquarters.

Several days passed before I called him. Though I had by this time found an apartment in a new development in Park Forest, Illinois – a short commute on the IC (Illinois Central Railroad) to Hyde Park – it would be some time before my wife and two children (ages 2 ? and10 months) could make the move from Russell.

In the interim two things happened that aroused my concern about my true sexuality. The first occurred the night I went to the former sailor's apartment for dinner. It was almost déjà vu of the experience I had had with the general's aide in Augsburg – but this time I resisted.

After dinner our conversation had gradually turned to matters of sex. He showed me a photograph of himself in his sailor uniform with a very large penis outlined on his left trouser leg. He then undressed and showed me an erection that was truly enormous. Much to his disappointment – and mine as well – I explained to him that I just couldn't have sex with him. Much as I desired it I thanked him for dinner and quickly left for the bachelor officer quarters – where I masturbated as soon as I found privacy in the latrine.

The other incident that occurred before my family arrived was of a different nature, but still something I'll never forget. It happened that there was another reserve officer recalled to active duty at Fifth Army Headquarters whom I had known while in ROTC at college. He had married a sorority sister of my wife's and had already found an apartment near headquarters in Hyde Park.

One night I got a call from him asking if I could possibly come to their apartment and baby-sit for their little girl. His wife suffered from asthma and he had taken her to the hospital and needed my help. Of course I agreed and came over as soon as I could. The child soon went to sleep in her crib. It was late at night and since I had no idea when they would return I took off my uniform and crawled into the double bed nearby wearing only my underwear.

Falling quickly asleep myself, I was later awakened in the middle of the night by the anguished father of the child. I couldn't believe what had happened. He was in tears as he told me his wife had died. Whatever had been done for her in the emergency room had failed. He was exhausted and told me only that he needed sleep and would have to decide what he should do the next morning to get her body embalmed and take it back to Kansas for a funeral.

Asking me not to leave he crawled into bed with me and sometime later I awoke to find myself in his embrace. Kissing me on the lips he called out her name. As I pulled away he seemed not to wake up, turned over, and nothing further occurred. We both awoke in the morning when the child began to whimper for attention and nothing was mentioned of the incident.

As far as I know my friend was straight – nice guy, a trifle nerdy, someone I respected as a fellow officer, but no one to whom I was sexually attracted. Despite this fact the event made me wonder what might have happened had I been of a mind to respond to his sudden kiss and rather violent embrace.

I must write about what happened when I was in Korea that made me further question my sexuality. When the Chinese entered the war, inflicting heavy casualties on our Marine and infantry divisions at the Yalu River, we infantry officers at Fifth Army in Chicago quickly received orders to proceed to the war zone in the Pacific.

Luck again came my way, as I mentioned in the previous chapter. When assignments were being made to us newly arrived officers in Taegu, Korea, rather than being sent to a combat infantry unit I was sent to War Crimes Investigation in Pusan – about as far away from actual fighting as one could get and still be in the war zone. There had been many massacres of prisoners by the Chinese and North Koreans as the front lines moved back and forth. Photos of prisoners with their hands tied behind their backs bore stark proof of these atrocities. Our assignment was to prepare evidence that would support possible convictions at future war crime trials such as had been held in Nuremburg at the end of World War II. (As it turned out a truce, with division of North and South Korea at the 39th parallel, ended hostilities and no war crime trials were ever held.)

Life in Pusan was uneventful. We officers lived in Quonset huts and there were several civilians working for the United Nations who shared our latrines and showers. The opportunity for sex with one of the civilians soon presented itself as both of us found ourselves achieving partial erections while bathing in the open showers. Though I knew I would have enjoyed giving in to his advances I hurriedly dried off and retired to my quarters. One evening, later on, we met on the grounds of our compound and talked for over an hour. The temptation to accede to his wishes for sex was great, but my fear of a dishonorable discharge if we were caught was greater. I did not give in and he eventually gave up on me. His civilian status made any risk for him much lower. Had he been a fellow officer with as much to lose as I, the situation would have seemed less risky to me.

I did engage in mutual masturbation with a married officer of equal rank to mine, but again I was not the aggressor and felt no shame whatsoever for doing what we did. We had met when we both attended a Christian Science Church service in Pusan. He had his own jeep and eventually we shared the privacy of that vehicle.

To be separated from my wife for long periods of time occasioned by two wars in which I served was more than I could bear without some sort of sexual contact with a human being. On rare occasions prostitutes were available, but fear of venereal disease was a sufficient deterrent for me. Being with another man seemed natural. I was doing much the same thing we boys had done growing up in junior high and high school and I had done on rare occasions with fraternity brothers in college.

When my tour of duty finally ended in Korea I returned to my wife and two children and resumed law practice with my father in Russell. It seemed wise to file for the office of County Attorney since County Attorney John Woelk, a Republican, was not running again and no other lawyer had as yet filed for the job. I had been absent from my hometown for most of the time since graduating from high school ten years earlier, and I thought that running for office would allow me to meet people and canvas the county, shake hands with prospective clients, and if elected earn a small salary on my own. My father had served as a Democrat County Attorney in his first years of practice and he encouraged me to file. Win or lose, it was an opportunity to get myself known, as a lawyer.

Up to then I had always considered myself an Independent, voting for the candidate I thought best qualified. Now I needed to decide in which party primary to file – Democrat or Republican. General Eisenhower, a man I greatly admired, had only recently declared himself a Republican and since Kansas was heavily Republican, my choice was obvious if I wanted to be elected. The filing itself got publicity in our two local papers. I soon had posters printed with my photograph, and handed them out to various stores, and with the help of my wife Sari, tacked them to telephone poles throughout the county.

And then the unexpected happened. Bob Dole, my high school friend who had just graduated from Washburn Law School in Topeka, also filed in the Republican primary. While I continued to campaign, my heart was really no longer in it. I was already a partner with my father, who was one of the three leading lawyers in town. Bob, a severely wounded veteran of World War II, needed the job and to his credit was an untiring and charming campaigner.

Ironically I had, myself, encouraged Bob to study law. As I recall, it was sometime in the spring of 1946. Kenny, Bob's younger brother, had gone to Michigan to bring him home from Percy Jones Army Hospital in Battle Creek. I vividly remember sitting with him on the porch of his parents' home. Bob was frail, and in low spirits. We were both recipients of the highly respected Combat Infantryman Badge and each of us had lost our closest high school friends. Although Bob's time in combat with the famous 10th Mountain Division was relatively brief, he had the misfortune of being seriously wounded as he bravely lead his platoon only a short time before the war in Europe ended in May of 1945.

As we sat together that morning I could sense how much it hurt Bob to be without the use of his right arm. To soldiers the wound that doesn't kill, yet is serious enough to get you out of combat and sent home, is called the million-dollar wound. To a star high school athlete, a college varsity basketball player, and a young man who one day would have been a respected surgeon, this wound was to Bob a catastrophe.

Seeing how depressed he was, I pointed out to him that he could have a great future as a lawyer. My visit was a short one, as his wonderful mother Bina had requested, but I left hoping the encouragement from another hometown veteran might have helped. In many books that have been written about Bob and his struggle to rise above his war injury, I found only one reference to a suggestion that he should study law. It apparently came from his highly regarded surgeon, the man who was able, by performing many operations, to permit him to hold a pen in his otherwise useless right hand. Whether or not Bob remembered my visit and suggestion that law might be a good career choice, I do know I suggested it and will never forget how terribly depressed he seemed that morning. Later I read in his memoirs that he felt ashamed of his body and didn't want to see any of his friends other than the Dawson brothers who ran the drug store where he had worked while attending high school.

Much has been written about our race for County Attorney and most is accurate. My family, however, was far from wealthy; I never had a car of my own until I was married; and I, too, worked while going to high school at numerous jobs – delivering flowers for the Holzer Flower Shop, selling clothing at the Virtue Clothing Store, pressing and altering clothes for Heffel Cleaners, setting type and writing copy for the Russell County News, cleaning my father's law office, and jerking sodas for the Russell News Stand in the Mecca Theater Building across the street from the popular Dawson Drug Store where Bob worked.

By the time of our race for County Attorney I had my wife and two children to support and it is true that some of my white shirts were sometimes frayed. It never entered my mind, however, that I had worn them to suggest in any way that I needed the job as much as Bob did.

Years later John Woelk, the outgoing County Attorney, was quoted as saying, "Dole used his war wound to the limit." Never once in our race against each other did I feel Bob used his war wound unfairly. He had to use his left hand to shake another's and he rightly drove a car with Kansas license plates bearing the inscription "Disabled Veteran."

Should you ever visit the imposing *Robert J. Dole Institute for Public Service and Public Policy* on the University of Kansas campus, you will see an accurate quote about our race correctly attributed to me: "How long was my day? I don't know, but it wasn't as long as Bob Dole's I'm sure of that." It was a statement I made to the writer Richard

Ben Cramer, when he interviewed me in New York for his fascinating book entitled What It Takes – The Way to the White House. Bob never made it to the White House, but he came pretty close. In my opinion he's a good guy and I will always consider him a friend.

Had I known ahead of time that Bob wanted to run for County Attorney, I would never have filed for the job. Though our race was in all respects friendly and surprisingly close (Dole 1,133, Ostrum 948), I have to admit that I somehow felt a bit less wanted in my hometown that I had before. Had Bob not run against me I would probably have won as the Republican in the general election that followed. Would I still be living in Russell, practicing law as my father did for over sixty years before his death at 84?

As someone once said, "When you come to a fork in the road, take it." I did. Later that fall I accepted an offer to join the Kansas Attorney General as one of his six assistants in Topeka. That soon led to my decision to accept employment as a corporate attorney with the Bell System. In more ways than one my loss to Bob Dole has made for a far more interesting life than the one I might have had if I had won and stayed on in Russell as a country lawyer.

CHAPTER NINE: Don't Ask, Don't Tell – Just Stay In The Closet

As a gay combat infantry veteran with two bronze stars (the second in Korea), battlefield promotions to First Lieutenant and later Captain, a record of escape after capture by the Germans, and with periodic army efficiency ratings never below superior, I was saddened, sometimes infuriated, during the debate over gays in the military as it unfolded in the news.

When candidate Clinton fervently pledged in his campaign that as President he would promptly issue an executive order lifting the ban, he got my vote. When he failed to deliver, went back on his promise, and asked the Joint Chiefs of Staff for their views on implementation, he opened a political debate he was destined to lose. What followed was a circus, with Sam Nunn and Bob Dole competing for ringmaster. Soon degenerating into a pep rally for bigotry, the Senate Armed Services Committee hearings were a sham. The radical religious right was afforded another fund-raising field day.

In May of that year I wrote letters to two Republican senators whom I personally knew – Mark Hatfield of Oregon and Bob Dole of Kansas. Telling them of my deep concern and describing my military record in World War II and Korea, I urged them to read the recent Randy Shilts volume entitled Conduct Unbecoming – Gays & Lesbians in the United States Military. Widely praised by critics as authoritative and comprehensive, this book showed that over the past decade the military had wasted a half-billion dollars chasing down gays and running them out of our armed forces.

Although I had seen and spoken cordially with Mark at a wedding in Washington the month before, my letter to him went unacknowledged. At least Senator Dole had the courtesy to reply promptly. His personal letter of June 17, 1993, read as follows.

> Dear Dean,
> It's a pleasure hearing from you, and I appreciate your frank, personal views concerning homosexual orientation.
> Your record of service in the U.S. military is indeed exemplary and I do not question that, like you, many gay individuals have served honorably in our military.
> The issue that we in the Congress are dealing with is whether or not openly gay and lesbian behavior impacts the readiness, morale, and unit cohesion of our military. Dean, your insights are appreciated.
> Sincerely,
> /Bob/
> Bob Dole

Then I learned of the duplicity of which my Kansas friend, and too many politicians, are capable. I discovered that several months previous to his personal note to me, Dole had authored a lengthy, printed fund-raising letter on behalf of the American Conservative Union. High-lighted on page one was this statement from Bob: "...we must fight the liberals night-and-day to prevent the advancement of their own radical agenda that includes: ... a lifting of the ban on gays in the military..."

So much for Dole's pretended objectivity. In his letter to me he deceptively implied that he would be weighing the matter fairly, but his mind, like Nunn's, was closed from the beginning.

After six months of front-page-headline fodder for every newspaper in the country, Clinton caved. His so-called compromise of "Don't Ask, Don't Tell" changed very little. You no longer need lie to get in, you just have to lie to stay in. This means facing almost certain humiliation and expulsion if you even accidentally breathe a word about a vital aspect of your very being. The debate's result was just a politically expedient way of continuing the ban, another insult to those Americans who happen to be gay or lesbian.

The military's argument for keeping the ban has become a litany, almost a mantra. Their stance is that openly gay behavior adversely impacts combat readiness, morale, and unit cohesion. Since privacy is minimal, sleeping and showering in close quarters will create sexual tension and possible aggression. Comrades in arms must be able to bond so closely they will be willing to die for each other. Many service men and women will not re-enlist if the ban is lifted.

Similar arguments were made and proved wrong when President Truman issued his executive order ending discrimination against blacks following World War II. An expensive Rand Corporation study, commissioned and later suppressed by the Pentagon, concluded that homosexuals can serve openly and effectively – provided the policy gets strong leadership from above. Analogous points about gays being security risks were laid to rest by a Navy study way back in 1956. Other countries like Canada, France, and Israel allow gays to serve openly and numerous large city fire and police departments have likewise integrated gays with no reported loss of effectiveness.

Fears about unwanted sexual advances wrongly brand all homosexuals as sexual aggressors. The same specter of unrestrained sexuality was raised to thwart women in the military, but to no avail. There, however, the tables were turned – heterosexual men being the potential predators and women the endangered ones. The answer depends on whether or not there is strong leadership from above. Regulations prohibiting sexual harassment should be equally enforced in all cases, regardless of gender.

The religious far right often argue that lifting the ban will give government blessing to what they believe is sinful behavior. Pointing out Bible passages that condemn homosexual acts, they selectively ignore other passages that carry equally severe rules for condemnation and punishment.

They would have the government legislate their views of morality – in no way agreeing that what consenting adults do on their own time is their business, not the military's.

As Anthony Lewis said in a column about the evangelical right entitled "Merchants of Hate,"

> ...It will be an intolerant America if they have their way: something like a Christian version of the Ayatollah Khomeini's Iran. Pat Robertson tells women: 'The husband is the head of the wife, and that's the way it is, period.' Dr. Steven Hotze, a Texas Republican who won party office with the help of the Christian Coalition, wants to execute homosexuals.

Disappointed as I am with my country's continued opposition to gays and lesbians in the military, I am optimistic that the U.S. Supreme Court will eventually find it unconstitutional on the grounds that it is a denial of equal protection and an infringement of the right to free speech. Many lower federal courts have already done so.

Gays have served honorably in the military in the past and will in the future. Former Senator and Republican Presidential Candidate Barry Goldwater emphatically said that there is no valid reason whatsoever for continuing the ban. "You don't need to be straight to fight and die for your country," he added. "You just need to shoot straight."

I can only hope for a lessening of prejudice and hatred toward gays. Many years ago Sgt. Jose Zuniga, the Sixth Army's Soldier of the Year, wearing a chest full of medals, stood before the television cameras in Washington and said that he was proud to be a soldier, and was proud to be gay. As more and more Americans find the courage to come out, there will be a change for the better in our society. When more mothers, fathers, brothers, sisters, close relatives and friends, even business colleagues, discover for the first time that someone they love, respect, or admire is gay, it is bound to make a difference.

I especially like what Anna Quindlen, the author and columnist, said in an op-ed piece in The New York Times some time ago.

> ...it's the power of one that really brings change... A veneer of tolerance atop a deep pool of hatred, distrust and estrangement is no more than a shining surface... The numbers [in last year's gay and lesbian march] in Washington were not as important as the faces, the sheer humanity of one person after another stepping forward, saying: Look at me. I'm a cop, a mother, a Catholic, a Republican, a soldier, an American. So the ice melts. The hate abates. The numbers, finally, all come down to one.

What happens next? Only time will tell.

CHAPTER TEN: Lessons From Childhood

As I look back on my writing thus far, the memories of a number of unrecorded but significant (to me, that is) events keep coming back to me. Four of them could be described as lessons from my childhood.

The first lesson I remember being taught was that I should never steal. It was summer and I was about five years old. My mother had taken me with her to shop for a few groceries at Roth's general store. While she was busy paying for her purchase I picked up a walnut from a large basket of them and slyly slipped it into my pants pocket.

Later that day she saw me playing with the walnut and asked where it had come from. When I told her, she explained that what I had done was wrong, that I had stolen the walnut. My punishment was to return the walnut to Mr. Roth and apologize for taking it without paying. It was a mortifying lesson I have never forgotten.

The second lesson I remember learning as a child was never to be cruel to an animal. One Sunday afternoon while playing in our yard with one of my young cats I discovered the principle of centrifugal force. Holding the cat by her tail I found I could swing her in circles over my head and it seemed like great fun – to me, that is, not the cat.

Suddenly my father charged out of our house. "Never, never let me see you abusing an animal this way again," he shouted. "This is how what you were doing must feel to your cat." And with that, he led me inside with his fingers painfully gripping my left ear. Lesson learned.

The third lesson I learned as a child was never to cheat. In third grade I had a teacher who was extremely strict and would publicly punish a student caught doing anything she disapproved of. We were having a spelling test in which there were several words I found difficult to remember. It occurred to me to copy them in ink on the palm of my hand. Being right-handed I simply read from my left hand when she called out a word that had given me trouble.

That trouble, however, was nothing compared to the trouble I found myself in when she caught me. She made me write on the blackboard one hundred times "I shall not cheat" before going home that day from school. I never told my parents what I'd done, but learned a lesson that never left me.

After returning to college following World War II, my wife and I enrolled in a beginning course in German. Sari had a seat right beside me and when we were writing our final exam of the semester I covered my paper and wouldn't let her see my answers. My lesson from third grade had never left me. I got an "A" in German and she got a "C". I think Sari thought my refusal to let her see my exam paper had been a bit much.

A few years ago when Richard and I were having breakfast at Sari's during our then annual family reunion at Thanksgiving, my grandson Anders was criticized by his grandmother for wearing his cap in the house – always either backwards or at a jaunty angle sideways. When he turned to me and asked, "Did you ever misbehave as a child, Grandpa?" I felt moved to relate the following (and fourth) lesson I had learned—and it still embarrasses me to tell it.

One day while walking home from kindergarten I picked up a tiny, solid gray-furred kitten with large yellow eyes – obviously a stray with no home. Before learning she was female I named her Elmer and never changed the name – even after she gave birth to her first litter of kittens in a lady's coat on my parents bed while the lady was attending a luncheon meeting of my mother's church circle.

In those days, the late 1920's, we had no indoor plumbing and only a two-hole outhouse in one corner of the garage. One dull summer morning with nothing better to do, I took the five kittens from Elmer's most recent litter and dropped them down one of the toilet holes. I can't imagine why I did such a thing. Curiosity? Some sort of scatological fascination connected to my older brother's semi-swear words often uttered (only in my presence) when he was angry – "Rectum, tailee, pee-pee, mussy"? The kittens could walk, were not fully weaned, but old enough to meow. And meow they did.

My loving and beloved grandfather Daniel Gross whom we called Poppa and my grandmother were visiting that weekend. Luckily for me, it was he who discovered the kittens on going to the outhouse. I immediately confessed to what I'd done; that I had had no intention of hurting them – just an unspoken curiosity in learning how they'd fare – in all that shit. Beyond a stern reprimand, my only punishment was to clean each kitten thoroughly and return them all safely to their mother Elmer.

But how could we retrieve them? With the help of Poppa I found a long board in the garage and nailed on plaster lath for little steps. This ladder-like device was lowered into the hole, but the kittens had not yet learned to climb. They meowed louder and louder. Eventually Poppa conceived the idea of using an empty grape basket with a length of clothesline rope tied to its handle. Eureka! An elevator.

Immediately upon lowering the basket to the filthy toilet waste, the grateful kittens piled in and were quickly hauled up to safety – and their baths at my expense. And never again did I even for a second consider putting kittens down a toilet hole.

(Anders couldn't stop laughing when he heard this story. And I don't believe he wore his cap in the house again – at least, not at Grandma Sari's.)

Proud father with John, baby Peter, Danny & Karna

Camping at Spirit Lake, Mount St. Helen's, before erutopion

CHAPTER ELEVEN: Movies – Theatre

When I was a kid, we had only one movie house in Russell, The Mainstreet Theater, as the sign read. It was for silent pictures. About the time talkies came along the Danielson family, who owned the Mainstreet, had it extensively remodeled and modernized, and added a flashy neon marquee that bore its new name The Dream Theatre. The most sought-after kid's job in town was selling popcorn, and my older brother Wilbur got that job, later becoming an assistant to Dale Danielson, the projectionist. Three years younger than Will (as he later called himself, always hating his given name), I more or less basked in his shadow at the Dream.

Movies I remember seeing were Our Gang, several Laurel and Hardy comedies, and lots of Westerns with cowboys and Indians. One movie that was sexually suggestive found its way to our screen. It was a movie starring Mae West surrounded by hunky guys (who were occasionally bare-chested). Miss West's enticing "Come up an' see me sometime" became a line we'd never forget. I got to use it the following summer when Joyce O'Brien, my classmate from kindergarten through high school, and I decided to play dress-up with her parents' clothes.

The O'Brien home on Main Street also served as Dr. O'Brien's veterinary office and the old two-lane gravel highway U.S. 40 ran beside it. (Joyce sometimes had a faint odor of the drugs her father kept to treat sick animals, but I never had the heart to tell her.) It was during the Great Depression and unemployed men wearing ragged clothing, hitchhiking across Kansas, were a common sight. They would stop at nearby houses asking for a drink of water, and often a meal, always offering to do some kind of work in return.

On the morning when Joyce and I were playing dressup a particularly handsome young hobo sat on the O'Brien porch eating a sandwich made for him by Mrs. O'Brien. Dressed in drag, I sidled up to him, rubbed against his thigh and uttered in my sexiest Mae West voice, "Hi big boy, come up an' see me sometime." He simply smiled, then laughed, but he didn't answer.

Should I have known? Even then?

Later, in high school, Joyce and I appeared in many school plays. We were colleagues on our school's state champion debate team, dated some, and finished valedictorian and salutatorian of our graduating class. She was beautiful and had the gracious bearing of her strikingly gorgeous mother who was Jewish. (I remember my mother often saying that Mrs. O'Brien was the only Jewish person in our town and that she was a living example of the wonderful people Jews were.)

In 1940 during our senior year at the University of Kansas high school drama festival we won best actress and best actor in a one-act play entitled Jacob Comes Home (which also won best play). It was about a Jewish family whose son had been arrested and beaten by the Nazis. I played Jacob, and Joyce played his mother. My make-up required a large, ugly scar across my left cheek made with putty. This I enjoyed doing and was the kind of thing, only second to dying on stage, that most thrilled me as an actor. (Decades later I was cast in an Off-off Broadway production entitled Autumn Illustrations where to great acclaim I finally got to die; it hasn't happened since.)

Joyce went on to college at Northwestern University, had a brilliant academic record, and was admitted to law school at the University of Chicago. She married a labor lawyer and they had two wonderful children. We were friendly with them when we were all living in Cleveland, where Joyce died of cancer. She had asked Sari for Christian Science help in the last sad days of her life. Unfortunately nothing helped. I still think fondly of her, her great parents, and her two outstanding brothers.

Acting and public speaking have always been a part of my life. In kindergarten my first audience appearance involved telling a simple little story about two mice – one from the city, the other from the country. Once on stage my legs began to shake and I was so frightened I couldn't utter a sound. As I was about to cry, Miss Leach, my beloved teacher, came out on stage, put her arms around me, and led me to the wings. A month later she scheduled me for a repeat performance. This time I felt no fear, told the story, and was henceforth healed of stage fright.

In college I auditioned successfully and appeared in several plays – Charley's Aunt among them. (It was during the run of Charley's Aunt that I first spoke to my future wife. I called her at her sorority for a blind date. Before responding she made an excuse to leave the phone. Later she told me what had happened: "Who is this Sigma Nu Dean Ostrum?" she asked a sorority sister. When told he was an actor then performing with the University Players, she returned to the phone to accept my invitation. It was our first date.)

In law school my defense counsel classmates often chose me to be their accused client in mock criminal trials. Never convicted I stood trial for every conceivable crime all the way from rape to premeditated murder. Acting in the trials was also an opportunity for me to associate with talented Yale Drama School students who found that our trials offered them excellent experience in improvisation.

In 1955 after resigning as an Assistant Attorney General of Kansas I joined Southwestern Bell Telephone Company. Sari and I sold our home in Topeka and moved to Kirkwood, Missouri, a short commute by bus to my office at 1010 Pine Street in downtown Saint Louis. Soon after the move Sari noticed a flyer for auditions for an upcoming production of the Kirkwood Theatre Guild. Knowing of my love for acting she suggested I try out. And I did.

The show was *Born Yesterday* and I got the male lead – the role of the uncouth, crooked, foul-talking Harry Brock. It was a memorable experience with one of the most-talented community theatre companies in the country. The female lead, Billie Dawn, was played by a talented young woman who was a member of Actors' Equity and whose husband worked for Monsanto Chemical. Had the director known me I might never have been cast in such a role against type. I loved playing a character so different from anything I'd ever done, and we received excellent reviews. My new boss, Mark Garlinghouse, Southwestern Bell's Vice President and General Counsel, and his wife Marjory came to see the show and expressed pleasure and surprise that I could play such a part.

While my work thereafter as a corporate lawyer for the Bell System was too demanding to permit acting in community theatre, I took advantage of every opportunity to be close to professional theatres in cities where I worked. For example, I sometimes ushered at the Alley Theatre in Houston, and personally met Margo Jones, Artistic Director of Theatre 55 in Dallas. She was living at the Stoneleigh Hotel, where I stayed while studying for the Texas bar exam.

Upon moving later to Portland, Oregon, I often traveled on business to San Francisco where I saw my first production at the renowned American Conservatory Theater (ACT). While in Seattle I was a founding fundraiser for Seattle Repertory Theatre and while in Cleveland I served on the Board of The Cleveland Play House. Later in New York I joined the board of National Corporate Theatre Fund (NCTF), an organization that raised corporate contributions for many of the leading professional regional theaters in the United States.

As retirement from the Bell System came closer the thought of pursuing a second career as an actor appealed to me. With the steady and enthusiastic encouragement from my partner Richard I enrolled in an evening acting class at the Herbert Bergdorf-Uta Hagen acting school (HB Studio) on Bank Street. Michael Beckett was my first teacher of scene study and after my divorce I soon found myself a member of his three-hour Sunday invitation only class. My classmates became like family and after my retirement from law practice in January 1985 I subscribed to *Back Stage – The Performing Arts Weekly* and began to audition seriously for acting opportunities in New York. Happily many came.

My first play was directed by Kate Harrigan, the granddaughter of Nedda Harrigan Logan with whom I served on the NCTF board and her husband Josh Logan the director of *South Pacific*, Mr. Roberts, and many other Broadway hits. The play was an Equity-approved showcase entitled *Parallel Lines*, written by John Harris and starring his partner Tom Connor. Its cast included several members of Actor's Equity and it had its premiere performance at Christ and St. Stephens Episcopal Church on the upper west side. The parish had commissioned John to write a full-length play on a topic of his choosing and their theatre company was well known for excellent professional work.

My supporting role was the homophobic father of a gay son struggling with his sexual identity. Though Sari and I were by then divorced, she came, with our middle son Danny to see the show. She was, as always, very supportive, and encouraged me to continue my acting.

Perhaps the highlight of our week's run occurred on opening night. After the show was over Josh Logan came with his wife Nedda to our dressing rooms. Taking me in his arms, he hugged me and said, "Congratulations, Dean. You are now one of us."

Much of the joy in acting on stage comes from the camaraderie with other actors. (See Appendix #4 for a few letters regarding my work.) (See photos.)

With our four children

With our nine grandchildren

Richard & Dean on a street in Greenwich Village

Richard & Dean following dinner at Serge's – 2006 St. Bart's

First visit to St. Bart's in 1992

CHAPTER TWELVE: The Year and a Half After The Outing

*B*y not facing up to the fact that I was a gay married man, my wife and I only postponed what finally happened – namely the events briefly related in the "Outed By My Children" chapter of these memoirs. Here is a more detailed – yes, and painful – account of the year and a half that followed that outing. It was probably the saddest, most stressful period of my life and these letters, both of mine and those from my loved ones, make it achingly clear.

First, the full letter from youngest son Peter at Ohio State University:

Dear Father,

2/1/77

I apologize for the lateness of this letter, but I'm finally settled here at school. And I hope to write you often in the future. School (the first 5 weeks were smooth) is beginning to get a little rough. In all of my classes we are finally getting into the meat. The introduction work is over. I try to think of my school day as a workday, where I must study 8 hours a day. Most of the day is spent with chemistry, English, and reading (Shogun right now). On my third theme I received a lousy C+. It was due to my careless spelling errors. The writing itself was very good, so the T.A. told me. I have no tolerance for careless mistakes, and needless to say I was really ticked at myself. But I'm here to learn, nobody is making me push myself, except me, and it feels pretty good. I am trying to defeat the voice in me that says I can't do it. I'm tired of giving up, and making excuses for myself. I don't want to be defeated and if I am, I had better give it my all. The time we spent together in New York really felt good. But at the same time I can feel a change in both you and Mom. Not only am I concerned about you as my father but as my friend. I have come to grips with the fact that Richard is probably your lover. I don't feel bad or hurt at this fact for you have taught me well & raised me to understand these things and accept people as they are. Don't falsely judge people. These ideals that you have instilled in me are probably the greatest things anybody has ever taught me, and I hope to instill them in my children.

As parents, Sari and you must come to some agreement, before you destroy each other. Decide what is best for you as individuals. I can't allow you to keep tearing at each other. This isn't right, and it does neither of you any good. Mom only sinks deeper into her Christian Science and you sink deeper into your guilt. Please understand that I am not condemning either of you. What's happening now has been lying dormant for years, and like a buried seed is beginning to germinate. Regardless of what happens, I will still love you as my friend and as my father, for both of whom I have the utmost respect.

I'm angry at myself for being so cold to you over Christmas, but I couldn't talk about these things at that time. This letter has been in the making for over a year. Please forgive me that it took so long to be a man and face reality. I can only speculate on how you must feel and what you're going through. My heart goes out to you. We are all so afraid and alone, it's time we crushed these wicked walls and put down this heavy load.
Love
Peter
P.S. Will you be coming through Columbus on your way to visit Grandma Helen?

On February 24, 1977, our middle son Danny, the varsity athlete in our family, wrote from upstate New York.

Dear Dad,
Whatever is running through your mind be sure and stick this in. I love you very much and that goes for Jackie. We always will. Love is something that is never lost. One might think it has gone but it can't leave. It's like an athlete who has an off day. He played a bad game of tennis like you and I do sometimes. That guy hasn't lost what he has. And that is playing a good solid game of tennis. It seems at times he's losing what he once had. But that is impossible.

What happens in our lives we all learn from. Life is learning new things. And we learn every day. If we didn't learn then life wouldn't be fun to wake up to every morning. What we might learn at the time might seem wrong or not in the best of interests. But it does have a purpose. Things happen for a purpose, a purpose to learn something that we need. And apparently you needed to learn something. That doesn't just go for you. It goes for Mom, Karna, Don, John, Meg, me and Jackie and Peter. Apparently we all have something to learn. We might not all learn it at the same time but someday sooner or later everyone will get it. Maybe our family was becoming too loose. I'd like us all to be closer. I view this all as something that had to happen – something that had to bring everyone closer together. Who would have thought this would be the way for bringing a family close together. It already has. That I know for the better. We all do things that might not be the best. I have something to tell you but I'd like to tell you face to face. And I am glad you went through what you did because I can get this off my chest.

Your marriage and our family is too precious a thing to leave behind. Families are the roots of mankind.

They should be preserved forever – and will. I know, and so does God.
Your Danny boy.
I love you dad and I always will.
And I'm crying too—

On March 2, 1977, our oldest son John, the architect, wrote the following letter that hurt greatly because much of what he said about my frantic civic activity during the Cleveland years was true.

Dear Dad,
Enclosed is the letter, my letter for all of us, which did not get sent. I still feel it defines the situation quite well. I thank you for calling Sunday. Since Peter's action I have been waiting for you to call or write.

There are many things I wish could have been different about our father/son relationship – perhaps now we can have the changes that could lead to it. I know that what I am going to write may hurt you deeply but I must let you know where my feelings are coming from.

For many years now I have felt you have never taken much of an interest in the members of your family as individuals – collectively yes, & in the moments of glory (plays, soccer, movies) another yes; but, as individuals I sincerely feel you have never sought us out. I know in my case there were many times I could have used your friendship and guidance. Often I asked myself why – was it your job, "civic duties", or simply your own absorption in your own life & its problems that kept you from working with ours. Over the past ten years, your greatness has shrunk before me. I saw a man who treated religion as a social occasion, a man incredibly concerned with the appearance of things rather than their substance, a man incredibly up tight about his physical appearance & aging yet one not willing to really exercise, a man who participated in all the 'right' causes and who was on the right boards without really being a part of them – a Science Museum with no knowledge of science or care to acquire any, a farm that's a suburban spec. development, horses that can't be ridden, gas to mow grass, fireplaces that take more heat than they give – I do not mean to sound like a mad man but I am desperately searching for the mind within the man – and I know there is one there.

I feel as if you have cut yourself off somehow – a clever mind, a very manipulating mind but not one that reads, reflects, or contemplates. You have played the lead role for so long in your life that I think you find it very difficult to consider others' thoughts and opinions.

All the time I worked in Cleveland I could not believe that we only had lunch together once in two years. These last few years have become increasingly painful. Whenever I have been with you I could sense an uncomfortableness, a near paranoia that shows in your face. You know I have come to not respect you in many ways for not dealing with your fears. How much this all has to do with being gay I do not know. I have known (of your being gay) since my encounter with Father Tom. The freedom of New York made your choice for you.

I beg you to get in touch with yourself, to relax and open up your mind. Think of whole systems and how your actions relate to them. Be sincere instead of pretend sincere.

Without your caring to know of my life and work it is next to impossible to want to be part of yours. Make the changes, find your happiness and
peace, and don't worry about the people who can't comprehend.

All my love & hope for you,
John

Whew! I grow weak in my gut every time I re-read this letter of John's. After Karna was married she once told me I should stop asking when her husband Don was going on to law school. It made me feel I should stay out of my married children's lives unless they came to me with their concerns. Obviously with John I made a huge mistake. Here is the letter not sent on January 24, 1977, but enclosed with John's letter above.

Dear Dad & Mom,
We are writing to express our concern for your happiness. For some time now, especially this past Thanksgiving and Christmas, all of us have sensed that you two are growing apart. We all, in our own experiences, have come to realize that human beings do change, and consequently, relationships between individuals will be affected. The reasons for your growing differences are both known and unknown to us. As your children, we cannot help but to wonder and speculate about them.

Underlying all the discussions we have had among us, though, is a sincere concern for your physical and mental well being as our parents, as husband and wife, and most importantly of all, as two individuals. We cannot remain painfully silent as we watch you two slowly wear each other away. In hope of averting deeper pain for all, we ask of you through talking, or counseling, or the courts that you please try and

> resolve your differences. Your marriage, as our parents, cannot help but be important to us, but your individual happiness is more important. Whatever the resolution, whether together or apart, we will always love you and remain, . . .
>
> Your Children

Luckily, Peter's understanding, loving letter of February 1, 1977, had arrived a month ahead of John's. I found it in my mailbox the morning after I had lied to Sari about my relationship with Richard.

In order to answer the many questions I knew my children were having, I felt it imperative that I visit each of them for a face-to-face conversation. I realized that my inability to admit to their mother that I was having an affair with Richard when she in effect asked if he was my lover had been the most selfish, dishonest thing I could have done. So despite my work I managed to make four weekend trips away from New York – Lansing to talk with Karna; Minneapolis for John; Rochester, New York for Danny; and Columbus for Peter.

"When did you first think you might be gay?"
"Why did you ever get married?"
"Who else have you had affairs with?"
"Did you really want to have children?"
"Can you change?"

The questions were many. I tried to answer each of them as truthfully as I knew how.

About this time my son John's brother-in-law Lanny Geismer lovingly wrote to me to suggesting I see a psychiatrist, and giving me several names and phone numbers as suggestions. My daughter-in-law Meg, Lanny's sister, and their parents were all like family to me (I'm still in close touch with their wonderful mother, Bobbie Geismer who lives in Cleveland). I didn't follow Lanny's advice to seek counseling, but I did decide that I should try to keep our marriage from ending.

The world I knew had fallen apart overnight; my life in two worlds had come to an end. The thought I had had that first night as Sari dropped me off at the Holland Tunnel had been of suicide. I knew now that such a thought, for me, was preposterous.

I still had a family that loved me; I had a job that made for a comfortable life; and most important of all, I knew that in the distant past there had been months, even years, when I had had no serious sexual involvement with another male. I truly believed I might do it again if I put my mind to it, and I decided I had to try.

But trying turned out to be exceptionally difficult.

When I told Richard of my decision he said nothing to dissuade me. He asked, however, that I return the key to his apartment that he had long ago given me. And I did so with great sadness. Still having apartments in the same building we continued to see each other, often meet for a drink after work, and go out for an occasional meal.

My strong feeling for Richard had not lessened as evidenced by the following note I recently discovered he had saved, along with the many birthday cards and anniversary notes I had sent him over the years.

Postmarked Greensboro, N.C. 4 May 1977, and addressed to "Mr.Richard Nagrodsky, 3 Sheridan Square, Apt.15C, New York, N.Y. 10014" the single page letter printed in pencil reads:

> My dear Richard—5:30 p.m.
> I just arrived at the motel and I am already homesick. I miss you much, probably more so since it will be over a week perhaps before I can return to New York. You'll never know how much you mean to me. You are the most thoughtful, loving person I have ever known. Washing & ironing that shirt really touched me. And the lunch & bloody Mary really hit the spot.
> I love you very much. Dean

That spring Karna, then working at Michigan State on her Master's Degree in City Planning while her husband Don was completing his Doctorate, had let Sari know of an opening for a sorority housemother at the University. Sari was interested and applied. She had always loved sorority life at the University of Kansas and her Gamma Phi Beta housemother had been very close to both of us. When she was offered the housemother job at Michigan she decided to take it, and she began to seek renters for our New Jersey farm.

Her decision to take this job meant that if there were to be any hope of us getting back together, I would have to convince her not to take it, but to come and live with me in New York. This in turn meant I would have to find another apartment, since it would be awkward for her and Richard to meet in the elevator. And if she were living with me in New York we would need more space.

The lease on my studio apartment was expiring that summer and before calling Sari, I found an exceptionally fine penthouse apartment in a beautiful pre-war building at nearby 45 Christopher Street – one bedroom with high ceilings, a stepdown living room with wood-burning fireplace, and a large wraparound terrace. The original tenants, an opera singer and her husband, were retiring to Florida. I immediately signed a three-year lease commencing August 1, 1977.

I then called Sari in Lansing, told her of the new apartment I had rented, and asked that she return home to me. She agreed at least to think about it. At that moment, I sincerely felt that our marriage could be saved.

The following letter dated June 29, 1977, from Karna soon arrived in the mail.

Dear Dad,

> Well by now I guess you know we kids think your timing stinks. But if your motivation to try to make a go with Mom is sincere then I want to be the first to give you my support. Peter's right – things will never be the same. Hopefully though some things can be a lot

better than they ever were. I want to trust you again & feel sure you're giving me honest answers to my questions – not what you think I want to hear.

Over the last few months I've come to see both you & Mom in a new light. I guess you're both a lot more human. Neither of you is as strong or good as I once thought – & neither of you is as independent and self-reliant. You've become a part of each other over the last 30 years – perhaps more so than either of you imagined. You've used each other, loved each other & raised a family – & probably have each had a very different conception of what your marriage has been, but only you two can say individually what it's been to you.

None of us kids should even attempt to judge that. I'm sure all of us have enough problems of our own to work out. I know it's easy for us to find fault & I guess it's because we don't want more hurt between you. So try to accept where we're coming from. We're talking to each other a lot more now & that puts you in a vulnerable position.

I love both you & Mom so much & think you've still got a lot to give each other. Be good to each other – whatever comes of this. Sorry this is so rambling but I'm just letting the words go as they come to me.

Love,
Karna

(This letter will always remain in my thoughts as dear Karna's "Your Timing Stinks Letter.") Then Sari's touching letter of July fifth arrived, with her answer to my proposal.

My darling Dean,

Needless to say, your telephone call the afternoon I arrived in Lansing took me by surprise.

I left home that morning, resolved to do the best I knew how to do at my new work here in Michigan; to leave everything else about my life in

God's hands; as I realized that was the only way I'd ever find peace of mind.

My life had always been so full with you and the children and yet somehow, I knew something was missing, unsettled or not right, yet I knew not what. I had wondered years ago, but never really dreaming, or being afraid maybe of the true reason – therefore not directly asking. Maybe, as we've said, it was a protection for both of us as well as our children.

If you are really sincere about wanting me to come home, to try and give you my support as your wife, I will feel as I do so, that it will be the first time I've really come home and been at home with you ever. I really can't think of a more wonderful feeling.

You sound on the phone as if you're more relaxed and free than you have ever been, and I'm sure that it can't help but be reflected in your work, living and attitude toward everyone, including your children. I am certain that they all are elated and eager to have us try to work out our lives in harmony.

As Karna said, it will really be fun to visit you and daddy now in N.Y. They too, all of them sensed N.Y. was never any part of their lives. I hope that they truly will feel that it is now.

I'm really looking forward to being home and with you again, Dean, and I hope you'll never regret your decision.

I love you dearly – Sari

Several days later, I was alone in my studio apartment when the telephone rang. The caller was Mary Merris, Richard's dearest friend with whom he had worked for many years. In a distraught voice she said she had just received a call from Richard telling her goodbye, and that he was committing suicide.

Mary, also my friend, knew of our relationship and asked that I go immediately to his apartment. I told her I no longer had a key, but would get the building superintendent to open the door and that I would immediately call 911 for assistance.

Fortunately I was able to contact the super. We opened the door and found Richard barely conscious on his bed. EMS arrived at the same time as Mary and another of Richard's close friends, Andre LaPorte, whom she had also called. Richard was rushed to the lobby and I rode beside him in the ambulance as we raced with siren blasting to Saint Vincent's emergency entrance. Mary and Andre followed on foot.

Luckily, dear Richard survived the ordeal and hours later, after they had pumped his stomach, he was able to walk with assistance. As a condition of being allowed to leave the hospital that night, he had to promise to see one of the psychiatrists suggested by the ER doctor who released him. He told me he would do so, but only on condition that I, too, would see the psychiatrist he chose. Of course I agreed.

We both thanked Mary and Andre for their great help. As they left for their homes, the two of us walked arm in arm the few blocks back to my studio apartment at 3 Sheridan Square where together we spent the balance of the night. I then and there resolved to keep Richard in my life – whatever happened to my marriage.

Every week for at least a year Richard saw Dr. Gary Portadin, who subsequently became one of our life-long friends. Thanks to Gary's help Richard became convinced that no person was worth taking one's life for. Gary knew that I had come to him only because of Richard's insistence. I enjoyed our sessions together, but he eventually told me there was no need to continue.

Sari and I had long planned a two-week trip to Scandinavia that August. Now more than ever, it promised to be a time we would have alone together, a time to talk without my having to rush off to work, and a time to reflect on where we'd been and where we might be headed.

My father's brother Andrew had once gone back to Sweden with his wife Dot. They had found church records of the wedding of my grandparents, Mary and Ola Ostrum, and even located one cousin and his children. Uncle Andy and the cousin discovered that they each had the same photo, taken during a prairie fire near Bunker Hill, Kansas – visual proof beyond doubt that they were related. The trip to Scandinavia was my chance to explore my roots and Sari, too, was happy and eager to go.

When Karna was a senior in Shaker Heights High School, we had participated in the AFS (American Field Service) program, in which a foreign student comes to live in the States during his or her last year of high school. Our student had been Liv Sand from Kristiansand, Norway, and our trip in the summer of 1977 was an opportunity to visit our Norwegian "daughter" and her Norwegian parents, and the Swedish doctor she had married.

We had an adventurous time traveling in Sweden, Norway, and Denmark. We made contact with my distant relatives, and with Liv's family. Her husband, Lars-Gunnar Gunnarson, took me to his gym where we played racket-ball and enjoyed showering and sweating together in the sauna.

During this time away I thought of Richard often, and missed him terribly. In a men's room at the world-famous Tivoli Amusement Park I had one quick sexual encounter with a Dane who touched me, at the urinal. Again, though I was enjoying sex with my wife, I found it impossible not to have it both ways. Nothing had happened in the sauna with Lars- Gunnar, but I had had to hide the beginning of an erection when he scrubbed my back. (Sari asked me years later if we'd had sex together and I was able to tell her honestly that we hadn't.)

Upon our return to New York I followed up on my promise to Sari to see a male Christian Science practitioner who had been recommended to her. She was convinced that I could change. As it turned out I soon realized that he, too, was homosexual and anything he told me about Christian Science's ability to make me exclusively heterosexual fell on deaf ears. He asked many questions about my lovers and seemed more interested in the size of their penises than anything else.

Sari and I were living in the penthouse I had rented in the Village. My next door neighbor Michael Harvey at 3 Sheridan Square had given me several planter tubs from his terrace and Richard had emptied the soil so I could move them with the help of John Falocco, another friend, to my new terrace. We had brought several pieces of furniture from the farm in New Jersey – an antique desk that had been Karna's in Shaker Heights and a fountain called "Turtle Baby" – and were soon making New York more like a second home. On one occasion we had Richard to dinner with us before he and I went to see a gay movie at the Quad Theater nearby. I knew my sexual orientation was still the same, but at least now I was being honest with my wife and children.

My resolution to keep Richard in my life is also evidenced by the following letter postmarked "San Francisco, Ca. 1 PM 23 Oct 1977" and mailed from the airport while I was flying to an annual Bell System legal conference being held that year at the Del Monte Lodge in Pebble Beach.

> My Dearest Richard, Sunday – enroute to San Francisco
>
> I am having real proof of why you insist on traveling First Class, or not at all. Although it was not 'ours', the champagne was passable before taking off. The brunch began with a bloody Mary – not nearly as good as we make – but acceptable. The sky is space blue & we're flying above beautiful white clouds. I simply miss you terribly and wish I could be with you. (The privacy of First Class is its real virtue. I'm alone with my memories.)
>
> When we sat together having dinner the other night and the tears streamed down my face as you described my possible future, I was crying because I knew you were telling me the truth of what may likely happen on my present course. 'Most certainly' is more accurate than 'may likely'. Above all I will lose the most precious thing life has ever brought my way – YOU, plus the beginning of an ability to live an honest life of which I can be proud – not ashamed – and happy because I'm

finally being true to myself. And if I lose you for the reason just given, I will also lose what may yet be left of a life – double though it was – with Sari. I did not tell you of her final comment the other night when we had our conversation following the discovery of my nude drawing of you. She simply said that she did not want to stay with me if she couldn't eventually have me to herself without sharing me with another. I replied that I wasn't seeing a psychiatrist to be changed, that I personally felt change was impossible, and that we'd give 'living in New York together' a try through the winter and just have to see where we came out by spring. She said we'd both just have to do a lot of praying. I replied that she could pray as much as she liked, but I wasn't going to – since my sexuality simply is what it is, a most important part of me, which no amount of prayer on my part will ever change. I know you're completely frustrated with my inability to decide what I should do and set my course without looking back. At least I'm getting closer to a decision – I only want to be sure it's a right one. That's probably too much to wait for, since no one can be positively certain in matters that are even 100 times easier to deal with.

At any rate I wanted you to know that I do love you – am in love with you – with all my heart. And also that it hurts so much not being with you that I simply have to do the next best thing and stay in touch. That brief telephone conversation yesterday meant more than I could ever express to you in words. I heard my lover's voice. He was alive, sounded strong, and said he missed me. It gave me the strength to go about living again. Some – in fact, a lot – of the heartache ceased. I don't know what I'd do without knowing you still loved me. You simply make life worth living.

Whatever happens, I try to know, will be 'for the best'. I wish I could be sure – at least you said that it would be so in your letter of Aug. 27th. I want to believe you. I guess I'd better, for you have your head screwed

on straighter than I do right now – & probably always have, and always will.
LOVE, Dean

Then without any warning I was stunned and surprised to receive the following handwritten letter from Richard, postmarked November 10, 1977, and delivered the next day to my downtown office.

My Dearest, Dearest Dean,

I'm afraid I'll never be capable of expressing in words my love for you. The most fragile flowers in the world, the soft sunrises and magnificent sunsets, the intense blue of your eyes, the few times you've shown anger with me; perhaps these wonderful things show a tiny bit of my feelings for you but there are not enough words to even come close.

I could never describe my delight in just looking at you, the smile within me when you would brush your hair back with your fingers or tell one of your funny jokes. Sometimes they were funny just because you were telling them in your own special way and watching you tell them wanted to make me take you in my arms and laugh and hold you and kiss you all over. There are so many, many things about you that are so special and bring indescribable joy; the way you smile, the way you move, the way you can be so gentle and tender.

My Dino you've made me so proud of you. I think back to when we first met and how you were always looking over your shoulder so nervous and afraid. You've come so far so many ways in our short time together. I hope you won't look back and decide to turn around.

So my love, please know how deeply my feelings go for you and realize also how impossible it is for us to continue seeing each other. It seems we want the same thing in life – to be together, but in different ways. You want us to live in one way and I in another. I guess all this time I misunderstood. Please forgive me for being such a fool but with all my heart I wish I could understand. I wish we could make each other happy.

I guess it's best if we just walk away from each other. You're handsome and charming and will meet someone who can accommodate himself to your life. You have many years ahead and with Sari's help they'll be the happiest ones of your life.

As difficult as it is to describe how much I care for you it's twice as hard to ask you not to contact me but this pain and misery is becoming more than I can bear.

My Dearest Dean – please don't forget me –

All my love,

Richard

Sari from her standpoint had expressed a similar feeling. On one of the walks we took together that fall she had told me she could perhaps tolerate an occasional slip on my part, but she really felt I should move away from the temptation of Greenwich Village.

After reading Richard's letter while still at my office, I wrote the following reply (dated November 11, 1977, 5 p.m.), stamped the envelope without mailing, and dropped it with Richard's doorman on my way home. By now my heart was really breaking. I loved both Sari and Richard, and understandably from their points of view, neither one wanted to share me with the other.

My dearest Richard,

Your beautiful letter is at my side. Only you have ever said such lovely things to me. Only you have made me free of fear for my gayness. And only you have given me happiness the like of which I've never known before.

As for searching for another it's just like me to try some day. But I have no present urge to do so and a certain knowledge that I could never, ever, come even close to finding what we've shared together.

As difficult as it will be, I promise <u>for your sake</u> not to contact you. While you are right that we can't agree on our respective life styles, I would be dishonest if I didn't confess to great ambivalence over what I feel I really want. At times I know I'm right, and again, I'm just as sure I'm wrong. The torment of going through periods of diametrically opposed conclusions is why I must never stop seeing Gary (the psychiatrist) until I find peace. Would that it could someday be peace and happiness together.

My prayer is that you will now be spared more pain and misery. Whatever you do, don't interpret my lack of contact as evidence of even the <u>slightest</u> diminution in my love for you. When those moments come when I feel I will die if I can't just hear your voice, or catch a glimpse of your proud, slender body, I must <u>make myself</u> realize that I will hurt you more if I succumb. I can only prove my love if I resist you. I know that now.

Richard, I will <u>never</u> forget you—simply because I'm in love with you my dearest. You have taught me well the difference.

All my love always, Dean

The frustration I felt was oddly similar to the feelings I had had when writing Sari the following love letter while stationed in Heidelberg awaiting my return to the States. (The letter is dated September 30, 1945, Sunday.)

My dearest darling,

This has been a strange day. I took 'off ' as I felt a little bum from a slight cold. I laid in bed until 11:30, ate dinner, & then took a long walk by myself. It's now 4 o'clock & I'm back here in my room. It's been the first I've had time to be alone for a long time & it surely helps to stop now & then just to see where you're going – what direction you're headed in. We live so fast most of the time a lot of changes can take place without noticing them. I'm not crazy, honey, I just have a good case of ETO (European Theatre of Operations) blues today. I don't mean that I'm unhappy, it's just that I want to quit all of this & come home & live my 'real life' with you so badly.

I haven't had any mail for four days now & I'm certainly hoping there will be some tomorrow. The mail gets tied up, it seems, whether there's a war on or not. Perhaps that accounts for the mood I'm in.

It doesn't seem possible that tomorrow's the first of October. Oh, darling, how I hope I might get home for Xmas. You can never tell what will happen, but at least I'm sure that I'll be on my way shortly thereafter. How is it going to seem to have all the responsibilities of a husband again, Sugar?

Honey, what I want more than anything right now is to be able to sit down & tell you everything I've seen & had happen to me & around me since I've been gone. It all puzzles me so at times that I just want to talk about it to someone & you're the only one I want to tell it to. I'm afraid you'll find me getting into spells like these occasionally, darling. I can't put it in writing, but I surely feel it inside of me. Remember all those letters I used to write when the going was tough & I didn't know whether I would get home again or not? Well, I tend to forget how terrible the war actually was now & it's only when there are days like today that I get to thinking of it all again. I can sit here & dream of all that's happened & all the swell guys I met who are now dead. It makes me want to do something for them & I feel so darned helpless right now as to what to do. Well, honey, I'll figure something out in time & when the time comes you're going to be right beside me to help me.

Better I shouldn't have written this afternoon, precious. Anyway, Sugar, if you don't know what I mean I'll try to do a better job of explaining when I see you in person. At least, I love you with all my

heart, darling, & don't forget you're all I have – you're my future, beautiful.
All my love always,
Dean

If you can remember that last night on the golf course at Benning before you left – that's exactly how I feel right now. Sweet dreams, sweetheart.

The golf course event was the first and only time Sari and I ever removed our clothing and had intercourse in a public place. It was pitch dark with no one in sight, and for me, a memorable experience. A few weeks before writing the Heidelberg letter I had also had my Augsburg experience. This was one of the things I wanted to tell Sari about, but upon returning home I never did. Would our lives have turned out differently if I had?

CHAPTER THIRTEEN: Last Year of Marriage

The year Sari and I spent living together in New York City grew more difficult as the months passed. Sari hoped, and I'm certain prayed, for my sexuality to change. For me it was impossible. Marriage counseling was not an option it might have been for a heterosexual couple. As our marriage disintegrated, I remained silent on the subject, as was my way. But Sari finally resorted to the only way she knew to communicate with me. In the fall of 1978 she handed me a six-page, handwritten letter as I was leaving the farm to return to the city for work.

My dearest Dean,

> Now that Peter has gone back to school let's talk about us. It seems as though there's never any real time for doing so, so I thought maybe I could write better.
>
> For nearly thirty-five years you've been taking care of me out of a sense of obligation, as you were caught up in a marriage not of your own choice. I think it's time you had your freedom to do just what Dean wants to do, without having to lie about where you've been or what you've been doing.
>
> I tried living with you for a whole year in New York knowing what was going on, but I realized last February when we were at Barb Duff's that you would never be happy until I was no longer with you. I accidentally overheard a conversation you and Margaret were having, not that you were being secretive about it, I just happened to be within hearing range. Margaret said something to the effect about you taking care of what you did (I don't recall her exact words) but I'll never forget your answer. "As long as I can do what I want to do and be me, I'll be fine." I knew then that if that was

the way you felt, I could never really be a part of your life.

I don't want you to live with me because of a sense of duty – I want you to live with me because you love me and enjoy being with me. If we don't have that in common there's no reason to live together as husband and wife. I've loved being in N.Y. with you, although at times I felt in your way and out of place, but I've learned to love N.Y... I'm grateful you let me learn a little about it, for I don't suppose, had I been on my own, I would have chosen to live in New York. But yes, it is quite a city.

But for someone never really to miss his wife when she's gone, never feel enough emotion to really want to kiss her, to share the things with her that he does when they're not together, why I guess there's no reason to live together. Not that a husband and wife shouldn't have some time by themselves – they perhaps appreciate the other much more when they're together again – and circumstances have certainly forced us to be separated a great deal – but when they are separated, or even together, for one to have the desire to always be with someone else doesn't make for a very sound marriage.

For some reason you chose to go along with my proposal – how it might not have been had I not said what I did in that K.U. stadium some odd 37 years ago – but you did go along. I bore our children, and they have been the finest any parents ever had the privilege of rearing, and now they're gone and the life of happiness together with the one I chose to live has gone up in smoke. At first I thought it would be hard to live by myself, but I realize I can do it. I'll be given the strength and love; my physical and spiritual needs will be met and satisfied, because God never lets us down. You'll have what you need and so desire too.

I have learned to have great compassion for you, and I hope you'll find in life what you're seeking. As they said in "Roots" last night on television, "Don't condemn a white man for all the evil he's done to the black man, just because he's white, but condemn the erroneous ideas, the wrong thinking and doing." This is what I've learned to do and accept over these months. I've tried hard to put it into practice – it isn't you as a person I've so loathed at times, but the idea of what you've been doing. I've learned to see and think of you as the same wonderful Dean I married, full of love, kindness, generosity, happiness, compassion, consideration, helpfulness, joy, hard working, principled, and to know there is no other. This is the real you I love.

It seems as though you'll be happier to be able to do just as you want, without having me in your way, and I won't be around to have the mortal me seemingly hurt. That's something I'm still working on, although I don't think it can affect me anymore now.

You'll feel better to have a little more breathing space, and I'll be freer to pick up the pieces of my life and try to reconstruct it to the best of my ability. I'm sure I'll make many mistakes, but I'll find a solution somehow.

I'll try not to bother you in anyway unless it's some crucial matter that I can't absolutely solve without your help.

If you want to give me a list of the dates as to when you'll be out of the city this fall, I might use the apartment for when I'm taking my class, if you don't have someone else there. Otherwise I'll drive back & forth or take the train. If I find I'm to be gone on a weekend & you'd like to come out to the farm, please do so – I'll let you know if & when I'll be gone.

One time you said we had always been good friends and that's not quite right. First, I loved you, and I thought you did me, but I would never have lived with my best friend as I have with you, and yet with my best friend I could have shared every thought and idea I have had, and this I haven't been able to do with you.

Thank you though for a wonderful, wonderful thirty-five years of sharing my life with you, even though there have been many ups and downs.

Thank you also for the opportunity of knowing and loving your father and mother. I have loved them from the bottom of my heart. Your mother is the dearest person I have ever known and I really feel she loves me as if I had been her own. There's nothing I wouldn't do for her.

I will miss your many moods, your telephone calls, your warmness in bed, the entertaining we did together, our running and walking, your gentleness, but to be separated will be better for you, to give you your freedom to do just as you please.

May God bless you always dear, and may you have my blessing for a happy, full, enriched life in every way.

Your loving and devoted wife
Sari
and just 'me' – love you Dean –
Sari

Although Sari's loving decision to end our marriage in many ways hurt, I realized she was right. She was giving me the freedom to live an honest life – a priceless gift for both of us as it turned out.

(Her plan to become a travel agent came to fruition; she was hired by an agency located in Oldwick, New Jersey, near our farm home, and before selling the farm and moving to be near two of our sons in upstate New York, she spent many years traveling the world.)

I insisted she stay with me in the New York apartment during the weeks she was in travel school and not burden herself with commuting. One evening I returned from work and found that she had packed her clothing and moved out. She had said nothing about the course ending that day, but had left a note on our bed.

Twas nice sharing your pad for thirty-five years. Have a glorious, happy, and joyous new beginning in the New Year. If you ever need help with anything, don't hesitate to call. Only good can come from all that's happened. There must be a blessing for the whole family. You'll always have my love.

Sari

The following February John and Peter's close friend Bill Warner from our Cleveland days visited Sari at the farm. His Norwegian wife accompanied him and Sari invited me to join them. After returning to New York I received the following letter from Sari, parts of which I couldn't believe were hers.

Dearest Dean,

It was lovely to have you home on Friday night. Bill and Kirstie enjoyed seeing you. They did have a wonderful time visiting Princeton. I do hope Bill gets in the Seminary if that's what he really wants. They are two dear friends.

I'm sorry I broke down. I lost and I'll have to learn to make the best of it, but I'll never believe what you said when you stated you were proud of being 'gay'. You have really been brain-washed, haven't you?

Why don't you put all of that energy into proper perspective and help in a worthwhile way? It's true there is a need for non-discrimination in housing, jobs, etc. – but there is a greater need to help those who want out of that way of life. You could be such a wonderful example and help to many if you would only let yourself.

We all have to see man as not heterosexual, homosexual, but as spiritual. When we can do this, man can claim his dominion over the material senses.

I don't suppose I'll ever cease to love you, as I have from the day I met you – and thirty-seven years is a good share of one's life, but I realize you want your freedom from me.

Applying for a divorce is the hardest thing I've ever had to do in my life. It hasn't come easy – so I hope you'll be happy and have what you want out of life.

Happy Valentine's Day – Love always, Sari

Reading this letter I felt sure Sari was must be seeing a Christian Science practitioner who had told her that I could be healed. To suggest that I had been brain-washed was not like anything she'd ever said to me before. Homosexuality is not a choice and it saddened me to think she now believed it was.

(Once while we were living in Cleveland Sari wanted to attend a Christian Science lecture and Peter, then a sophomore in high school, and I accompanied her. By this time I had given up on my effort to remain a member of her church and had joined an Episcopal church in Cleveland Heights. Avoidance of medical treatment had always been anathema to me and fortunately Sari never objected to my insistence on vaccinations for our children. My only fear, as they were growing up, had been that one of them might become ill during the many times my work took me away from home and that Sari would delay in having them seen by a doctor. Luckily they were all healthy.

Religion had never played a prominent place in my life. Sari had given me a Bible and Mary Baker Eddy's Science & Health with Key to the Scriptures after our marriage, but I left them both in England before crossing the Channel and entering combat in Normandy. It was only after being sent to Korea in 1950 that I decided to give Christian Science a try.

As I have written before, when I told Sari and Karna goodbye in Seattle as my troop ship was leaving for Japan, I truly believed it was goodbye and that I might never see them again. Later, while sitting in a jeep parked in front of a Protestant Church building in Pusan, I looked up and saw a placard reading "Christian Science Services." I looked at my watch and realized a service was then in progress. I went in and listened to the two readers. The lesson-sermon that

Sunday was "God Is Our Life." For me it was an epiphany. I suddenly realized that God was my life and therefore I could not lose it. From that day to this, I feel healed of the fear of death.

That day in Cleveland, at the Christian Science lecture, Sari was seated next to me with Peter on her other side. The lecture had ended and the speaker announced that he would answer questions written on slips of paper earlier distributed by the ushers. Sari handed me a couple slips as an usher came by our aisle. As the lecturer got to one last slip he had placed aside, he became visibly disturbed. His face flushed as he read the question. "What does Christian Science say about homosexuality?" And what followed was an angry diatribe about the evil of homosexuality. He ended by saying that its practice would put such a person on the path to hell.

As our children grew I sometimes wondered if any would be gay. I was shocked, saddened, and worried that the question might have come from my son – rather than, as I learned years later, from my wife. As we drove home from that lecture I exploded in angry denunciation of such a wrong and stupid response. We had many openly gay friends who were actors and technicians at the Cleveland Play House. Sari had probably thought the lecturer would say that Christian Science could heal one of homosexuality, not that it was some sort of mortal sin.)

Upon the advice of our lawyer friend Dick Stevens in Cleveland, Sari consulted a prominent law firm in New Jersey and asked that the partner Dick recommended represent her in applying for our no-fault divorce. I used the Davis Polk firm in New York and the two lawyers arranged for an amicable division of our property with alimony to be paid by me as long as Sari lived, unless she re-married. I insisted that all contents of our farm home be Sari's and not counted in the division of our property; that she live there as long as she wished, only giving me my 20% share if she ever chose to sell. She later asked that I return the antique desk and turtle baby fountain that we had taken to the New York penthouse. This left me with none of the material things we had accumulated during our marriage. It hurt that she would ask, but I didn't object. Above all else I wanted to be certain our children could never question my fairness. Twenty-five years later I still pay Sari alimony and frankly enjoy writing that check. She deserves every penny of it and I've not missed one month since our divorce was granted.

As for the divorce itself, the court in Flemington, New Jersey, set Monday, September 30, 1980, for our hearing. (It was the same courtroom where the Lindbergh kidnapping case had taken place.) Our youngest son Peter accompanied his mother to the courthouse and I came alone. Her lawyer presented our agreement to the judge and he then asked if we had any objections. The whole procedure was over in a few minutes and Sari, Peter, and I left together.

All of us seemed on the verge of tears. Sari handed me a long letter she had written the previous Saturday, and asked if I was now going to marry Richard. Taken aback, I replied that there was only one marriage in my life and that I would always love her. It was a painful occasion for all three of us, but I had no doubt that we had done the right thing. I knew Peter agreed and I hoped Sari would one day feel the same way.

I placed her as yet unread letter in my briefcase, we all hugged goodbye and I drove away, heading back to work in downtown Manhattan. That afternoon, before leaving my office for my Village apartment – now my only home – I opened and read my wife's last letter. It was five-pages long, handwritten, dated Saturday night, September 28, 1980.

> To my dearest Dean,
> Once my husband,
>
> As I drove home tonight from being with Mother, the moon rising over the hills was more beautiful than ever. It was lovely too when Jackie and Cody were here, and I taught them the song of 'I see the Moon, the Moon sees me, the Moon sees someone I want to see.' I had to struggle with the last line, but I finally finished it. I had sung it so many times during

the Second World War that it brought back too many memories. Now you've been gone as long as you were during the war. Jackie taught Cody where the moon and stars were, and he kept pointing to them every few steps. He is so precious.

When you receive this, the legal separation will have taken place, as you wished, and you will have your freedom that you have so desired these many years. If I felt like the bottom had dropped out when the first papers came, you can't imagine how I felt when the letter arrived asking me to appear in court.

I really don't know why I'm writing except that as your wife I guess I kind of feel obligated to send you one last letter, although to you I'm sure it makes no difference.

I take it that perhaps you went to see my mother at Tenacre, as she had a box of Godiva chocolates that it took her some time to remember where they'd come from. It was kind of you. She always has loved you dearly.

I had quite a time tracking our marriage certificate down, as I never did know what happened to ours. Since I got two copies, I thought you might like to have one just to see what it looked like. I think it's rather pretty. It only came in today's mail. I ran across a letter written to us on our second anniversary from the minister, Clark Neale Edwards, wishing us the very best. I wonder if he's still alive?

At the moment I felt very, very alone, and hope I'll get through Monday morning in one piece. I guess nothing is worth crying over though. I pray to God that I'll be given the strength to carry on.

It was a wonderful, happy thirty-seven years, and thanks for sharing part of them with one who loved you deeply. May you have many more –
Love from your wife –
and to you – a friend,
Sari

As I read this letter, my eyes were full of tears. But I didn't cry. An important new chapter in my life was about to begin.

Border Collies Lucy and Mattie

CHAPTER FOURTEEN: Significant Others In My Life

Who have been significant others in my life? That is, aside from Sari. No other woman, that's for sure. But there have been four men.

First was Bill Shirkey. We met by accident. One morning while I was waiting at a bus stop in Dallas, he stopped his car and offered me a ride. It was across the street from the Stoneleigh Hotel where I was living during the several weeks prior to my family moving down from Saint Louis.

(This was the hotel where I met Margo Jones, artistic director of Dallas' "Theatre '55" and known for giving new playwrights their break. One play she produced, Inherit the Wind (the story of the Scopes trial), went on to Broadway and subsequent fame. Every New Year's Eve she changed the year in her theatre's name. I attended her productions often and it was in Dallas that I became involved with professional theatres in cities where I lived or worked. Ms. Jones later died from carbon tetrachloride poisoning while lying on her recently cleaned carpet reading a script.)

Bill Shirkey was a handsome, out-going guy with a dazzling smile. He was an extremely successful stockbroker who had married his SMU (Southern Methodist University) sweetheart. On the morning of our meeting we talked of my family and my new job with Southwestern Bell Telephone Company. Before dropping me off at my office he suddenly asked if I would be interested in attending a party being given by his friend Stanley Marcus. He said it was a get-together for couples that had recently returned from vacations abroad. I said that I would love to go and only later learned that the host was the head of the famous Neiman-Marcus department store.

After the Marcus party both Bill and I sensed that our attraction for each other was sexual and we soon found occasion to engage in mutual masturbation. My living alone in the Stoneleigh Hotel made meetings convenient and we soon became close friends. (Never a gambler, I even invested $100 in penny Uranium stock he recommended. After it more than doubled in value I used the proceeds to buy a stylish Nieman-Marcus suit, but never played the stock market again).

For a small town boy from Kansas, Dallas was an exciting place.

After my family joined me in our new home Sari and I occasionally played bridge with Betty and Bill, exchanged dinners, and attended social events together. The most memorable one was a Neiman-Marcus fortnight, where the beautiful young actress Grace Kelley was given a fashion award. Dress that night was black tie, so it seemed odd to us that a young woman at the Stanley Marcus table was wearing a rather too simple, short black dress.

After an elaborate dinner and much dancing, the ballroom suddenly faded to darkness. There in a single bright spotlight was the lady in the black dress standing before dark curtains hiding the musicians who accompanied her. She began to sing. Never before or since has a voice so moved me. There stood the "little sparrow" in the flesh – the world-renowned Edith Piaf. Though I neither spoke nor understood French at the time, her signature "*Non, Je Ne Regrette Rien*" is still with me.

Maybe it was infatuation, but following Bill Shirkey's and my first sexual encounter I discovered that it was possible to fall in love with another man – truly a revelation in my life. The attraction was so powerful that he was often in my thoughts and a joy to be near. As it turned out, the affair lasted only a few months because I wasn't the only guy in Bill's life. Soon thereafter I was sent to New York City on a six-month stint to work on an AT&T task force studying the possibility of having customers own their own telephone equipment – this being then an unheard of thing.

We closed our house in Dallas, rented a lovely old furnished home on Lloyd Neck across the lane from a house the Lindbergh's had lived in following their son's kidnapping and murder in New Jersey. Our half-year in New York was a joyous time. Ice-skating in January, picnics at Jones Beach in the spring, good schooling for the older two children, and our youngest son had our dog, a Dalmatian we had air-shipped from Dallas. (Peter, our fourth child, though conceived there, wasn't born yet.) Weekend trips to New York City included the ferry ride to the Statue of Liberty, the Empire State Building, and a visit on board an ocean liner at the Hudson River Piers.

There was one disadvantage – the horribly long commute to work at 195 Broadway in downtown New York City. On the best days it took three hours going and coming. I decided that should I ever again work in New York, we would have to live in Manhattan.

Within a few months of our return to Dallas I was hired by Pacific Telephone & Telegraph in San Francisco to be their first in-house General Attorney for Oregon. It was time to say goodbye to Bill Shirkey. He and Betty eventually divorced, but Bill remains a loyal friend to this day. He occasionally calls, has met Richard, and now lives in New Mexico.

From 1957 to 1963 while we lived in the Pacific Northwest – first Portland, then Seattle – my life was full of challenging work, water and snow skiing, some sailing, and family camping trips. On only rare occasions when traveling to San Francisco or New York were there passing sexual encounters with men and no involvement that in any way threatened my marriage.

(Here might be a good time to relate that I have never been in any way attracted to sex with a minor. And when a minor myself, I was never molested by an adult. Only once was I even aware that an adult was interested in having sex with me. It occurred in Hays, Kansas, while I was seated in a large auditorium at a high school music competition waiting my turn to play a clarinet solo. The man sitting next to me extended his hand to my thigh. I immediately moved to another seat and told no one about it.)

In late 1963 we moved to Cleveland where I was hired as Vice President and General Counsel of the Ohio Bell Telephone Company. My mentor Walter Straley had three years earlier made me the first Vice President and General Counsel of the newly-formed Pacific Northwest Bell Telephone Company. After being told by Straley that he felt I should one day be a Bell Company President rather than "just an in-house lawyer" I had briefly taken a line management job as General Commercial Manager for the State of Washington. He assured me that I would shortly be promoted to General Manager in Oregon, and if I did well, a company Presidency could well follow. A horrendous ice storm struck soon thereafter devastating many forests and Walt himself was briefly hospitalized with what used to be called a nervous breakdown. My decision to chance a competitive run for a company presidency suddenly seemed less wise and when offered the Vice President and General Counsel job in Ohio I accepted.

Our ten years in Cleveland were in many ways the highlight of my Bell System career. The company President gave me carte blanche in enlarging my in-house legal department and as I related in an earlier chapter, I took advantage of the opportunity to hire the first black lawyers in the Bell System. He likewise had no objection to, and in fact encouraged, my involvement in civic activity.

The egotism that Lucille New observed in junior high school was fed by the numerous leadership roles I accepted – first, chairman of the Board of Managers of the Downtown YMCA, later chairman of the Case-Western Reserve University Board of Overseers and ex-officio trustee of the university, board member of The Cleveland Play House, trustee of the world-renowned Cleveland Orchestra, member of the executive committee of the Cleveland Bar Association, president of the Cleveland Chapter of Phi Beta Kappa, and finally president and later life trustee of the Cleveland Museum of Natural History.

The years in Cleveland were tumultuous years for our country. On November 22, 1963, while Sari and I were inspecting the upstairs bedrooms of our newly purchased Shaker Heights home, the former owner's maid suddenly interrupted to tell us that our President had just been shot. (I later learned that Dr. Robert Daniel (Bobby) Stewart, best man at our Christmas 1943 Birmingham wedding, had been in attendance in the emergency room at Parkland Hospital in Dallas when President Kennedy was wheeled in. Small world?) Two more assassinations followed: Dr. Martin Luther King, in April 1968 in Memphis; and Bobby Kennedy, the following June in San Francisco. After the King assassination Cleveland experienced days of rioting in its Hough area, as did Los Angeles in Watts. Chapter Five contains an account of my civic activities during these turbulent times.

The Cleveland years were also full of major family events – high school plays and sports; three high school graduations; three college entrances and graduations; several professional theatre roles and a movie for our youngest son; and two beautiful garden weddings – for our daughter and for our oldest son. A sadder note was my father's sudden death from a heart attack at age 84 and our subsequent concern about my mother's loneliness in Russell.

These, too, were the years that our country was involved in the Vietnam War, and violence was a common occurrence on many university campuses. Our daughter was attending the University of Kansas where the student union building was burned; our oldest son, draft age, was on campus at Washington University in Saint Louis where I attended a noisy student anti-war protest while visiting him. And at nearby Kent State in Ohio two sons of a company colleague were shot by Ohio National Guardsmen.

When American forces extended the war further by invading Cambodia I wrote John Erhlichman (yes, the John Erhlichman) a personal letter telling him of the frustration we were all experiencing during these sad times. (Long before his involvement with Richard Nixon, John and his fine family had been among our closest friends in Seattle.) His prompt answer saying that the invasion was necessary to protect our left flank did nothing to lessen my concern about the horrible losses both sides were suffering. (Although I am not a pacifist, my military years have brought me close to being one.)

And the second "significant other" event in my sexual life occurred during the Cleveland years. I fell in love with 28- year-old Art Thomacheck (not his real name) and it occurred quite accidentally.

As a respite from the demanding work of my job I had enrolled in an evening portrait drawing class at the Cleveland Institute of Art. Located in University Circle near the Cleveland Art Museum and Severance Hall, the home of the Cleveland Orchestra, the Art Institute was conveniently halfway between my downtown office in Erieview Plaza and our home in Shaker Heights.

The live models were fully clothed and usually older people. I loved drawing and our teacher was excellent. The two-hour class provided a complete escape from the frantic pace I was otherwise involved in and I thoroughly enjoyed it. Toward the end of the semester, there was an exhibit of work being done by the teacher's full-time students. One oil portrait done in the style of Rembrandt particularly appealed to me. The subject was an extraordinarily handsome young man with dark features and a somewhat brooding face.

When I told the teacher how much I admired the painting, he replied that it was the work of one of his best students and that its sale would be most helpful to this student. He gave me the student's name and I obtained an address for him from the registrar's office. It turned out to be the address of a building in the process of being demolished. Later I tried once again and was given another address. This time the building was intact.

Finding the correct apartment, I knocked on the door. It opened, and there before me stood the subject of the portrait I had admired. He smiled warmly as I described my mission, but told me the painting was currently in a show on the other side of the city. He said he would be pleased to sell it and named a price I immediately agreed to.

He showed me his studio, a simple room where he slept. We felt a mutual attraction, and we quickly became intimate friends. That fall I commissioned him to paint a portrait of our youngest son Peter as a surprise gift for my wife Sari. He eventually became a part of our family.

Upon moving to Cleveland, Peter had seen a production of *Winnie the Pooh* at the Curtain Pullers, the Cleveland Play House children's theatre, and asked his mother if he could take acting lessons. The following fall he starred in *The Brave Little Tailor* and was later cast as the messenger in *Waiting for Godot* (a production of the professional company). Thereafter he was cast in one show a year and the Play House family became a part of our lives.

The resident acting company and the technical staff included several gays. Two couples were role models of longterm gay relationships and they and other straight cast members were often guests in our home. Never will I forget being told by one of the gay actors who knew of both my friend Art Thomacheck and how much I loved my wife and family, "You have the best of both worlds." I had to agree with him.

Eventually Art painted portraits of my wife, all our children and myself as well – the latter taking an exceptionally long time to finish since it allowed us to be together for over an hour each sitting. He often came for meals in our home and I even cut his hair from time to time, just as I had always done for my three sons. His Halloween costumes were amazing and he was in attendance at both our older two children's garden weddings.

When Peter was hired to play the role of Charlie in the movie entitled *Willie Wonka and the Chocolate Factory*, he and his brother Danny, a star varsity soccer player at Shaker Heights High School, were the only children still living at home. After I took Peter to Munich for the first two weeks of filming, his mother replaced me for the several months that followed. During this period Danny and I were alone at home, with Art as a frequent visitor.

A fabulous cartoonist in addition to his many other artistic talents (such as partnering the principal ballerinas of The Cleveland Ballet), Art did a series of drawings of our family pets (a bird, a cat, and a bowl of tropical fish) watching our Basset Hound, Abigail, bake a disastrous birthday cake for Sari's upcoming birthday in Germany. These drawings, now framed, hang in a prominent place in Sari's upstate New York condo.

Suddenly one evening, several years into our friendship when I stopped by his studio after work, Art told me he had met a young man and was ending our several-year affair. Both of us knew there was no possibility of my ever leaving my wife and family and that separation would eventually happen. It was heartbreaking for me to be told he had another, but I knew he was right in being honest. Tears flowed from our eyes as we made love, there and then, for the last time. Still close friends, we stay in touch and occasionally reminisce about the wonderful times we spent together – proof again that one can continue to love another person, as I still do my wife, without physical involvement.

Subsequent to Art's and my sexual parting, two other men living outside of Cleveland came into my life as work took me to other parts of the country. One, a young Episcopal priest, divorced from his model wife, who served in a prominent parish in New York City, and the other a married, high-ranking executive with a Canadian corporation headquartered in Montreal. Both are still friends and both know Richard and enjoy a friendship with him.

Toward the end of our decade living in Ohio I was asked by the President of Mountain States Telephone Company in Denver if I would consider moving there and establishing their first in-house legal department. He was a Christian Scientist who had once helped me fly my son Danny home to Cleveland from a Colorado Christian Science summer camp after a cut foot became infected and required medical attention. Our family loved skiing in the six years we spent in the Pacific Northwest and after considering the subject with Sari I agreed to a Colorado move provided AT&T's Vice President and General Counsel would approve it. "No way," was his answer. "When you next move it will be *east* not west," he told me.

About this time Peter had used some of his movie money to buy an Appaloosa mare from Kansas, named Princess. We later discovered that she was in foal. A handsome stud colt named Joker was eventually born and we were soon boarding both horses at a stable where Peter was taking riding lessons and doing dressage. The decision was then made to sell our lovely Shaker Heights home and move to Waite Hill Village, farther east. We found and remodeled a small farmhouse on property with pastureland and a huge old but well preserved barn with many stalls. We all loved the country and had many friendly neighbors who also had horses. We boarded a donkey and even saw an occasional red fox crossing the road followed by her offspring.

In little more than a year, the call came from AT&T to move east as Vice President Regulatory Matters for Western Electric (the manufacturing and supply arm of the Bell System). My new boss would be the highly regarded Vice President & General Counsel of Western, Steve Fletcher, a Mormon who neither drank nor smoked, but had no fault to find with those who did. At this juncture the Bell System was defending itself in a major FCC proceeding looking toward the possible divestiture of Western Electric.

The decision to leave Cleveland was not an easy one. It meant another move for Peter, who was in his junior year at University School. The move would be less hurtful for Danny who had graduated from Shaker High and would be attending Principia College in Illinois the coming fall. All things considered – increased salary, a clear step up the corporate ladder, and the chance to go even higher – the position was too tempting for me to turn down.

The move to New York necessitated resigning from several civic posts as well as preparing an application for admission to the New York State Bar. Leaving Cleveland was likewise hard for Sari. Letters we received when the announcement of our move appeared in the press on March 15, 1974, are testimony to the place we had made for ourselves in the Greater Cleveland community. (See Appendix #5 for some of these letters.)

Would these letters, complimentary as they were, have been written had the writers known I was gay? We'll never know, but at least I hope so.

By this time Peter's interest in horses made it unthinkable that we would buy a new home without a barn, and pasture land. Our search for real estate ended with a house in Hunterdon County, New Jersey, near the village of Oldwick. We named it Hound Hollow Farm, and painted the name on our truck that we used to pull the horse trailer. The forested countryside was charming, including a nearby brook. The road to the property wound up high hills from which one of our neighbors could see the top of the World Trade Towers.

To avoid the commute I decided that, like many Wall Street lawyers, I would keep a small apartment in the city and return home to Oldwick on weekends. With the help of AT&T I found a studio apartment on Sheridan Square, in the Village. My new Western Electric office at 222 Broadway, across from St. Paul's Chapel, was a rapid subway run away; and I already knew the Village as an exciting place to live.

At the new farm home in New Jersey our architect son John helped in the design of a large, high-ceilinged living room with a huge fireplace addition. We later built a swimming pool and added a barn with room for hay, a tractor, a truck, and a car. That first spring Karna and her husband were living in Afghanistan teaching co-ed high school English with the Peace Corps. Our first grandchild had just been born in Kabul and they invited Sari and me to visit Afghanistan and see their baby, Jason Dean.

My new job at Western Electric and our serious involvement in the FCC proceeding in Washington, as well as a threatened Government anti-trust suit, made vacation for me unthinkable. Sari went by herself and had a fabulous time touring this ancient country and seeing our first of eventually nine grandchildren.

While she was away I met Richard Nagrodsky. Not at a bar, not on the "cruisy" streets of the Village, but sunning on the rooftop of our apartment house with many other residents on a delightful afternoon in June of 1974. Several weeks previously we had noticed each other on the elevator when I was with a real estate woman who had just shown me the seventeenth floor studio apartment facing Seventh Avenue that I rented.

Now on this sunny Saturday afternoon a group of drama students from New York University were noisily reading a play near to where I was lying. Having seen the "elevator" guy also sunning on the other side of the roof, I picked up my beach towel, walked across to a vacant spot near him, and asked if he minded me joining him.

Rather shyly he told me he had no objection. I've always found it easy and enjoyable talking with interesting strangers and still do. In the next hour or so we exchanged names and I learned that he was a graduate of Parsons School of Design (as was my closest cousin Helen), that he was a freelance illustrator, and that he had a studio facing Barrow Street on the fifteenth floor of our building. I told him of my work with the Bell System, that my wife, the mother of our four children was in Afghanistan visiting my daughter and our newly born grandson. I mentioned that my boss and his wife were picking me up later that afternoon to drive to the Larchmont Yacht Club for dinner with another couple who had been close friends when my family lived in Texas (he was now the Vice President and General Counsel of New York Telephone Company).

As I was preparing to leave the sunroof to get showered and dressed for the evening I asked Richard if he would be interested in coming with me to my apartment to see some of my Cleveland friend Art Thomacheck's wonderful drawings. He said he would like to and we went down to my studio on the seventeenth floor. Nothing physical occurred between us, but I'm certain we both knew it was a possibility, and more likely, only a matter of time. When Richard asked if I would like to come by his studio for a nightcap after returning from dinner, I readily accepted his invitation.

Much later that night, after returning from a delightful evening with my friends, I rang his bell and found him clothed only in a robe as he opened the door. It was June 29, 1974. Like most gay couples that end up in long-term relationships we count that night – our first sexual experience – as our anniversary.

Years later I learned that before our meeting, Richard had been told by his friend Dezia, a psychic, "You will leave the person you are now with and you will meet a married man with whom you'll have a long relationship and be very happy." While I've never much believed in psychics, we both agree that Dezia was right.

During the three years following our meeting I began to see more and more of Richard. Just as with my buddy Art, in Cleveland, our friendship was never kept a secret from my family. I actually felt that the life I was leading made for me again the best of both worlds. In fact, it was a dishonest double life and was beginning to take its toll on my marriage.

CHAPTER FIFTEEN:

My Shame For Dissembling

*W*ithout question, I have been guilty of dissembling – secrecy – on numerous occasions in my life. Now, on reflecting back, I feel a deep sense of shame.

In the beginning of my marriage there was no dishonesty. I truly loved Sari (still do). My hundreds of letters written during my years away in the military told her exactly how I felt. In no way had I married and fathered children to screen my homosexuality. The eventual realization that my lifetime attraction to my own sex was an obstacle to my happy marriage became evident to me only after our move to Cleveland in 1964.

With Art Thomacheck (see "Significant Others in my Life") I began the first affair wherein I could no longer deny my true sexual orientation. "The best of both worlds" gradually became a "double life" that was completely unfair to Sari.

I never told her any outright lies because I was never asked. But dissembling began in earnest. I was too cowardly to tell her always where I had been and what was happening. I now believe she knew, by that time, that I was gay, and that we somehow both chose to pretend that all was well. Her deep faith in Christian Science must have convinced her that things (my sexuality) could be changed if she prayed enough. The eventual move to New York and my insistence on keeping a studio apartment in the city to avoid a long daily commute, then set the stage for my meeting Richard.

Unlike many gay men of my generation I never felt or believed my attraction to my own sex was wrong or sinful, or that it was any kind of sickness. I felt it a natural and good part of my very being. As I matured I never felt the least bit homophobic and was “closeted” only because society required it. Never did I think of my marriage and my fathering of children as any kind of cover. I loved and wanted a wife and family and have been greatly blessed to have them.

As years passed I also found that I needed to, wanted to, and found joy in acting on my in-born attraction to those of my own sex. It finally became impossible to have it both ways. The double life I was leading only ended when my own sons had the courage to insist that both their parents face reality.

Earlier I wrote of the four significant others in my life in addition to my wife. I now feel I must write about Sari. How lucky I was to have her as my wife, what a loving mother she has been for our four children, how difficult it must have been for her to come to the realization that she had married a gay man, and most difficult of all, to realize at last that I would not (could not) change.

I have no doubt that Sari still loves me. Whether she can truly forgive me for the wrong and pain I have caused her, I may never know. Some days I feel terribly guilty to have lived so long not telling her of my sexual liaisons with other men. I had neither the desire nor the courage to bring the subject up for discussion. I probably knew it would mean an end to our marriage and I honestly (selfishly) wanted it both ways.

But the best of my gay world only came with meeting Richard. And it came to fruition as a result of the chance given me by my sons to admit the truth at last about my sexuality. Even then, as I’ve already written, I at first tried to turn the clock back, asking Sari to return from Michigan and try to make our marriage work.

For the hurt I’ve caused my wife, and children as well, I am sorry. I have no right to ask their forgiveness because I don’t deserve it. The double life I tried to live was wrong.

What lesson is here for others? Perhaps it’s as simple as trying always to be honest with your loved ones.

CHAPTER SIXTEEN: My Life With Richard

*I*n retrospect my life with Richard began with our first meeting, June 29, 1974 – the afternoon I placed my beach towel next to his on the roof at 3 Sheridan Square. I was still a married man and would continue to be one until the date of Sari's and my divorce on September 30, 1980. What began as an affair evolved into a being-in-love and finally into a deep and lasting love that has grown stronger by the year.

After the divorce Richard kept his studio apartment to use as his artist atelier and moved in with me at 45 Christopher Street. Our first vacation together was a one-week trip in 1981 to St. Martin in the Caribbean. Our second was a two-week trip in 1982 to Morocco. During the second week of that trip we stayed at La Mamounia in Marrakech, in a hotel room with a terrace that overlooked a huge swimming pool surrounded by gardens. Five times a day the Muslim call to prayer was heard, and in the distance was a breathtaking view of the Atlas Mountains.

On February 3, 1982, one of our last days at La Mamounia, I wrote the following note and left it on Richard's pillow.

Dearest Richard,

We are about to complete our two-week Moroccan vacation. I want you to know how much I've enjoyed it. Being with you is most of the time like being with myself. You are now so much a part of me that I can't imagine living with-out you. Your quiet nature makes me feel that I have the comfortableness of complete privacy even when we're together. It's a rare quality in a friend. In a lover, it's even more precious.

Very simply – WOW.

Thank you for being you. I'm a very lucky and happy person.

Dean

What I felt as I wrote, and what I still feel today, was the peace of living an honest life. (My deep love for Sari and our children has never changed and I will always be grateful to Sari for giving me the freedom to be myself.)

It was on this vacation that we met Michael and Margaret Korda. I had noticed them wearing riding clothes on our flight from New York to Casablanca. Days later on our first night in Taroudant at the beautiful La Gazelle d'Or, we were among a few guests in the dining room but had not met.

When our main course arrived Margaret leaned over to our table and said, "Be careful of the bones, the fish has lots of them." What a unique introduction to a couple that soon became dear friends.

Both Michael and Margaret were avid horse enthusiasts and rode daily. They also frequented the large swimming pool, where Margaret, Richard, and I sunbathed. Michael lay off in the shade writing Queenie (finally published in 1985), a novel inspired by his uncle Sir Alexander Korda's marriage to Merle Oberon.

The Kordas came to Marrakech and were also staying at La Mamounia, where Michael suddenly became seriously ill with food poisoning. As soon as he recovered enough to travel, they returned to the States. We had exchanged New York addresses and that fall we received an invitation to Michael's fiftieth birthday celebration at The Four Seasons restaurant. And what a party it was. Many guests, and celebrities everywhere.

After dinner everyone moved to another private room where a large two-by- fifteen-foot banner hung across the stage. HAPPY BIRTHDAY, MICHAEL it read, followed by equally large letters. LOVE, RICHARD AND DEAN.

"Richard and Dean?"

"Who are Richard and Dean?" several guests were asking.

Soon a large chrome-plated Harley-Davidson motorcycle was rolled onto the stage – a gift to Michael from his boss at Simon & Schuster. Following the presentation speech and a warm and funny thank you, Michael mounted the beast, started its engine, and revved the motor to maximum pitch.

As it roared to everyone's laughter I turned to Richard and said, "Oh my, I've been outed again – this time in public!"

I had come close to acknowledging my sexuality at work in 1980 after Sari's and my divorce. My new boss George Cook (successor to Steve Fletcher as Vice President and General Counsel of Western Electric) and I were sitting together in his office. When the business matter I had come to discuss was finished, George casually remarked, "I guess the reason for your and Sari's divorce must have had something to do with her religion, and different lifestyles."

"Yeah," I hedged. "That's probably right."

He didn't press the subject, and ended the conversation by saying that both Sari and I were highly regarded – that everyone wished us well. Sometime after coming to Western Electric in 1974 I had learned of the company's published nondiscrimination policy that included sexual orientation, so I had no fear for my job.

Although my job was never in jeopardy, years after retirement I did learn that my gayness was probably a factor in my not being promoted. While visiting George and his gracious wife Edith in their Garden City home one summer I was telling them both about how much I had enjoyed our years together at Western. When George became my new boss, I also mentioned how much it had meant to me to have been told by Mark Garlinghouse, the AT&T Vice President and General Counsel, that I had been one of three considered for promotion to Steve's job – the other two being George who got the promotion, and George Ashley, then Vice President and General Counsel of New York Telephone. From this I inferred that Don Procknow the President of Western had been given a choice.

Immediately George reacted. "This isn't true," he said. "Garlinghouse told me you never got the promotion because you were gay."

Realizing how much this hurt me, George later that week called me to say that on reflection he believed it was not Garlinghouse but another high-ranking officer at AT&T who had said my gayness would prevent me from getting the promotion.

I happened to mention this incident when talking later with a retired Western labor lawyer and he immediately said, "You probably have a discrimination case."

To me a lawsuit was unthinkable, but out of curiosity I did arrange a lunch with Don Procknow and George Cook where I specifically asked Don if he remembered being given a choice among three lawyers when George was hired. He said he could only recall George Cook being recommended and since he knew him well as his first Vice President Regulatory Matters, he was pleased to have him back again.

And it pleases me to relate that some years after my retirement in 1985, AT&T itself had an openly gay Vice President and General Counsel. "Things are getting better for gays," as the wife of my Seattle mentor Walter Straley once said.

Immediately upon my retirement from Western, AT&T hired me to counsel other company lawyers whose jobs were being eliminated as a part of the anti-trust suit settlement breaking up the Bell System. Having served in four different regional Bell companies plus Western Electric, I had many acquaintances throughout the United States and greatly enjoyed helping younger lawyers find new jobs.

(I used the proceeds from this final work for AT&T to remodel our tiny, but efficient kitchen in our apartment on Christopher Street. When we met, Richard knew nothing about cooking. But tired of Sloppy Joes and my boring dinners of steak, potatoes, and iceberg lettuce, he soon learned to cook. He now has the deserved reputation of gourmet chef and I confine myself to baking and desserts. We love entertaining friends as well as both our families from time to time.)

Retirement has been a joy. Unlike many of my colleagues who left the Bell System and either continued to practice privately or joined large, prominent New York law firms, for me, thirty-six years as a lawyer was enough. It was no secret that one of my retirement endeavors would be theater. Upon retirement as a trustee of the AT&T Foundation I was given a beautiful piece of calligraphy that begins, "To Dean G. Ostrum, who is retiring from AT&T to pursue a promising career in the theater..." The promising career in theater predicted by my colleagues fell short of Broadway, and even off-Broadway, but my theater interests have never waned.

For many years now I've been an active member of the Amateur Comedy Club in New York City. Founded in 1884 this private club is now the oldest continuously performing theatrical company in the United States. Though "amateur" appears in the name, quite a few of our members, like myself, are members of Actors' Equity, and most of our major productions are professionally done.

Membership consists of no more than 125 men and we have a sister organization, the Snarks, who produce two majors each season and whose members are often indispensable to technical work in set-design, sound, costuming, and lighting. Attendance at our 100-seat theatre in Sniffen Court, a mews on East 36th Street in Manhattan's Murray Hill District (now listed in the National Register of Historic Places) is by invitation only. The club dress code is black tie on weekends and jacket and tie for other performances – quite different from the blue jeans and T-shirts now occasionally seen at Carnegie Hall.

In the years I've been a member of the ACC my participation has included stage manager for *The Fantasticks*, production manager for Joe Orton's *Entertaining Mr. Sloan*, and actor in *Camping With Henry* and *Tom, Some Assembly Required, Our Town, The Gang's All Here, Dirty Linen*, and *You Can't Take It With You.*

Our club roster lists all active members together with the names of their spouses. Many members are single, but two actives, myself included, now list the name of their same-sex partner. Yet another example of how "things are changing for the better?"

Richard, in addition to my acting, has also encouraged me in two other retirement endeavors – calligraphy and the study of French.

My interest in lettering began in a high school mechanical drawing class, and as soon as I retired from lawyering I enrolled at the New School and over several years took every calligraphy course offered. Through a contact Richard made for showing his paintings we have both become long-time artists with the Swain Galleries in Plainfield, New Jersey. As gallery calligrapher I receive commissions and my work, with borders done by Richard, is always a part of the gallery's annual Christmas Miniature Show.

As artists Richard and I have long shared a working studio. First in his Greenwich Village apartment at 3 Sheridan Square, then in SoHo at 11 Grand Street. Since the year 2000 our studio has been on Fulton Street, two blocks away from the now non-existent World Trade Towers. (Though often passing through the World Trade Center on our way to work, we luckily were in Italy staying at the Grand Hotel Quisisanna in Capri on 9/11.)

My study of French began at the French Institute and continued later (for six years) at Hunter College. Senior citizens of New York City can audit any course where there's room, and pay only a minimal registration fee per semester. While at Hunter I have also taken courses in acting, theatre directing, advanced expository writing, and I'm now studying Italian.

Another joy in my retirement years has been finding a home at the Church of Saint Luke in the Fields. Situated on an entire block on Hudson Street between Christopher and Barrow, this high Episcopal Church has beautiful music and liturgy, and a welcoming hospitality for families, all races, and gays and lesbians. On my first Sunday there as a visitor I was greeted by a former high school classmate of my son John in Shaker Heights, Ohio.

"You're Dean Ostrum," he said as he welcomed me at the coffee hour. "My mother was chair of the women's committee at the Cleveland Museum of Natural History when you were president."

I immediately felt at home and thereafter made many friends who have often come to dinner at our home. One such occasion is particularly memorable.

Late on a Friday night in 1981 the Church of Saint Luke in the Fields caught fire. As fire trucks were arriving with sirens blasting Richard and I stood on our terrace watching flames and smoke pouring skyward on Hudson Street. Live television news bulletins soon confirmed the worst. My church was burning. By daybreak only three walls including the building's front were left standing. All else, including the adjoining meeting hall, was a smoldering ruin.

We wondered if our three Saint Luke dinner guests scheduled for that Saturday evening would be with us. All were active members of the congregation and deeply involved in all facets of its ministry. Reverend Gene White, a handsome young black priest who often celebrated the Eucharist; Peter Hawkins, a brilliant scholar who taught at the Yale Divinity School and often preached; and Frank Tedeschi, an especially close friend who trained the altar party, was often Master of Ceremony in procession, and who as Intercessor had a show-stopping voice as he chanted our prayers.

When the doorbell rang at the appointed hour, I opened the door and all four of us hugged and shed tears together. (Years later Gene died of AIDS, Peter moved to Boston with an endowed chair at Boston College, and dear Frank continues to serve on important holy days at our restored church in Greenwich Village.)

Immediately following the fire Saint Luke's began to rebuild. Services were held in the school gymnasium, and by 1985 the building of a beautiful new edifice designed by

Hugh Hardy was completed. Like all parishioners I knocked on doors in our building and the outpouring of support from friends in the Village was amazing. This all happened during the first horrible years of the AIDS crisis and Saint Luke's soon became the home of Saturday evening suppers conceived and made reality under the leadership of Bill Boyd, a close friend who later died of AIDS, and Dan Ade. (Dan Ade later became a priest, served as St. Luke's Vicar, and is now Rector of a church in California.)

At a Saint Luke's coffee hour in early 1985 I saw a flyer asking for hospice volunteers at Saint Vincent's Catholic Hospital in the Village. By this time the AIDS crisis had reached pandemic proportions and many of Richard's and my friends had died and were dying.

My volunteer work at Saint Vincent's Hospital soon began (more on this subject in a later chapter) and lasted for more than five years. It only ended after I lost eight patients and found need for a break. The fear of the AIDS virus was at first so great that only two funeral homes in Manhattan would accept a person's body. And as for funerals, Saint Luke in the Fields was nearly overwhelmed conducting them. In one three-month period our Priest Molly McGreevy remembers doing forty-five funerals, sometimes two a day.

In the twenty years that I have been attending services at St. Luke's my involvement has grown. At first I was often asked to read one of the lessons at the long Sunday morning service. Although I respectfully turned down Rector Ledlie Laughlin's invitation to become a vestry candidate, I soon found myself recruited by my friend Cindy Beal to serve on the altar as an acolyte. Eventually being licensed as an ecclesiastical assistant to offer the chalice, I have found service on our altar guild extremely satisfying. The high-church atmosphere at St. Luke's – beautiful vestments, lots of incense, a fine professional choir, and brilliant organ music – offers me great solace, to say nothing of what it does to complement my love of theatre.

Altar service at St. Luke's continues to this day and one of our priests recently told me that at eighty-four I was probably the oldest acolyte in the diocese. Truthfully the torch can get pretty heavy when the Gospel reading is a long one, so I've gotten permission from the clergy to let it rest on the floor. As yet no one has noticed. Or if they have, they've not complained.

Thanks to medical advancements, an AIDS diagnosis need not be a death sentence, as it was in those early years. After my divorce in 1980 and at the beginning of the crisis both Richard and I got tested for the virus. We were negative and have remained so. Before learning the good news, my greatest fear had been that I might have infected my wife. If such a thing had happened it would have devastated me. Fortunately, I have never had a sexually transmitted disease of any kind. Though some may have a natural immunity to the HIV virus, I believe that my disinterest in anal intercourse may have saved my life.

Appaloosa Jack, Abigail and Frieda

CHAPTER SEVENTEEN: The Fourth Significant Other

As I've written before, Richard and I share a deep and lasting love that has grown stronger by the year. But we have had our ups and downs – the only serious one being a four-year affair that came close to ending our time together. This then is the story of the fourth significant other in my life. To this day he remains my friend, but our sexual involvement ended years ago. Our meeting happened accidentally.

I started to write about this in the preceding chapter, "My Life With Richard," but at that point in my writing I simply couldn't stay on target. It's still difficult to write about. But here goes. Our meeting occurred the evening of September 28, 1994, in Paris, on what by then had become for me an annual fall trip.

But let me go back a few years. Prior to my first visit to Paris in 1991 I had been studying French for several years, auditing the same beginning and intermediate courses (called *French in Action*) over and over again at Hunter College. Each lesson consisted of a film episode, much like a soap opera, with many interesting, diverse characters. The setting was France, most of the time Paris. Having become somewhat proficient in speaking the language – understanding being another matter if the person spoke rapidly as most of the French do – I looked forward to visiting Paris – following in the footsteps of the actors who played Robert and Mirelle in *French in Action.*

A penthouse neighbor of ours had recommended a small hotel on the Left Bank as a clean and affordable place to stay. It was the "no star" La Louisiane at 60 Rue de Seine in the heart of the Sixth Arrondissement. Nothing fancy, the beds had old, lumpy mattresses, and free breakfast included only brown bread, no croissants. Not wanting to spend the money to go with me, and certainly not interested in staying at such a *bon marché* hotel, Richard generously suggested that I not go alone. He further suggested that I invite a close mutual friend of ours who was gay and a member of my church.

When I mentioned this to the friend, David, during coffee hour at church the next Sunday he said it sounded great and that he would soon let me know. Early the next day he called to say he wanted to go. We would share a hotel room and take off on the same flight from Newark the following week.

When we checked into La Louisiane the single room I had reserved had to accommodate the two of us. This was no problem. Not surprisingly the first night together we masturbated before going to sleep. David was a sweet, gentle guy, nice looking, and completely accepting of his gayness. Richard and I had sunned nude with David on our terrace, and liked him a lot.

The next morning we left the hotel before daybreak and took the funicular-vertical metro up to Montmartre to witness the rising sun from the highest elevation in Paris. At Sacré Coeur there was one person praying and the tourists had yet to arrive. Here David told me he had AIDS, and that the joyful ejaculation he had experienced the night before had been his first in many months. (David died on February 23, 1994, a few months after giving a grand, black tie, fiftieth birthday party for a hundred friends. On our penthouse terrace wall we have a small stone pedestal that he gave us. On it sits a tiny stone angel with folded wings. That little angel reminds me of David.)

The year following my first Paris visit with David I returned alone and again stayed at La Louisiane. By now I knew the owner who told me I would always have a room because he remembered seeing my 7th Armored Division patch on the uniforms of soldiers who had driven the Germans from his boyhood home in Normandy during World War II. At the time he had been only twelve years old. I often visited one hotel staff couple that lived together, never married, and who later became parents of a pretty baby girl.

Paris was like a second home and every September found me at La Louisiane catching up with my French friends and making new ones.

This, at last, brings us to the accidental meeting with my fourth significant other.

My plane departed JFK on Thursday evening, September 27, 1994 – the kind of overnight flight we now make every effort to avoid. It allowed me to check in at La Louisiane as soon as a single room was vacated and to take a long nap before going out for dinner. Fall is also the time of *haute couture* fashion shows, and hotel rooms are scarce. That year I was given a third floor single with a nice view of the garden courtyard. After several hours of much needed sleep I bathed in my tiny bathtub with its hand-held shower, shaved, dressed and ventured out to find a place to eat.

On my first trip to Paris David and I had visited Edith Piaf's grave in *Cimetière du Père Lachaise.* (It brought back memories of the Nieman-Marcus fortnight in Dallas, when my wife and I had mistaken her for hotel help – until she sang.) Afterwards David suggested we dine at Brasserie Lipp across from Les Deux Magots on the Boulevard Saint Germain, a short walk from our hotel. He said they were renowned for their cassoulet, a dish I had never tasted. (I later looked it up in the dictionary – "a traditional casserole of Southwest France consisting of beans slowly baked with various kinds of meat and often a confit of duck or goose.") It was delicious.

On this night of September 28, 1994, only seven months after his death in February, I decided to go again to Brasserie Lipp for cassoulet, reliving our fun time in Paris toward the end of his far too short life. Leaving the hotel I walked first to the famous Saint Germain de Pres church, lit a candle for David, and then walked across the cobblestone square to Les Deux Magots. The sidewalk tables were crowded with happy, noisy people. I then crossed to Brasserie Lipp. It, too, was crowded. I glanced at the menu, saw their special cassoulet listed, and asked the headwaiter if they had a table for one.

"Je regrette, Monsieur. Pas ce soir."

Disappointed, I strolled across the side street heading for some postcard kiosks outside a cigar store. I always mailed a card to Richard on my first full day in Paris. Finding the card I wanted, I walked around the kiosk and came face to face with a tall handsome guy in jacket and tie.

"Hi," he said smiling.

"Hi," I said back.

He was an American from San Francisco, in Paris for the Fabric Show, and had a dinner date with business associates at the Brasserie Lipp. He said they had yet to arrive and confessed that he had noticed me looking at the menu and followed me to the kiosk.

"How about a nightcap?" he said.

"Great," I replied.

I gave him my address and room number at La Louisiane, truthfully thinking I'd probably never see him again. Around nine thirty that night my telephone rang and the concierge informed me that Gibson Mann was waiting in the miniscule lobby. I asked that he be sent up and he soon appeared at my door.

Gib is thirty-one years younger than I and told me that night that he had always been attracted to men older than himself. I told him about Richard, my more than thirty-six years of marriage to a woman I still loved, my four children, and my many grandchildren. We found talking with each other easy and enjoyable. Gib had been married briefly, but had no children. He said he looked forward to meeting Richard and someday all of my family. He also said he was sharing a Paris hotel room with his woman partner in the clothing design business.

When it later became apparent that we were mutually interested in having sex, I confessed that, for the first time that afternoon, I had shaved my testicles and hoped it would not put him off.

"On the contrary" he replied, and immediately asked for my razor to do the same. This accomplished, we proceeded to spend a pleasant night together in my single bed. Thereafter we saw each other as often as possible in his few remaining days in Paris.

Here I should make it clear that Richard and I have never discussed monogamy. Likewise, we have never discussed having an open relationship. We have always taken one day at a time, enjoying fully our time together, and being lonesome for the other when apart. (On rare occasions we've engaged in a threesome with another guy.) We have always tried to be honest with each other, recognizing that there are times when we may be attracted to another. When I've told Richard that I never make the first move, he replies, "But you're always available."

At least in the case of Gib, he was right.

Upon returning to New York I told Richard of our Paris meeting, that Gib lived in San Francisco, how much I liked him, and that I had invited him to visit us when his work brought him to New York. I had told Gib of the annual dinner party Richard always gives for about forty of our closest friends on January second, which happens to be my birthday, and suggested he would be welcome. And as it turned out he came.

After the birthday party on January 2, 1995, we had Gib to dinner with just the two of us before he returned to California. I was hoping for a threesome, but it didn't happen. I had fallen in love with Gib, told Richard I loved them both, and hoped for the best. The next few years were painful, especially for dear Richard. He didn't want to share and soon said he didn't want me even mentioning Gib's name in his presence.

The distance between New York and California made it difficult to be with Gib, but we did manage to see each other on occasion. Eventually he met each of my four children, their families, and Sari. On one occasion he met me in Wichita and helped me trim and tidy up my parents graves in Bunker Hill, Kansas. I believe my children were surprised and somewhat shocked that I was seeing Gib – Peter especially indicating disapproval. They were proud that

Richard and I had been together for such a long time; they liked both guys but wisely stayed clear of giving advice.

A lot of what I found attractive in Gib were the things he had done in his life that were completely different from the way I had lived. He was an athlete, a powerful swimmer, and a varsity basketball player whose father had been assistant head coach at Arizona State in Tempe. At eighteen he became a guide for Colorado River Grand Canyon white-water rafting trips. He knew how to do construction work of all kinds, and flew his own single engine Cessna Turbo 210. And he wasn't just a jock. On the sensitive side he studied art in college, designed clothing, and was working for Sierra Design and planning a new line of upscale outdoor clothing with his woman partner when we met.

One spring I went with his Berkeley housemate, an older man just a few years younger than myself, on a two-week white-water rafting trip through the Grand Canyon with Gib serving as one of several rowers. Richard said I was crazy to go since I couldn't swim, but it was a breathtaking experience I'll never forget. Perfectly clear nights, brilliant stars, scary rapids, wildlife, an occasional rattlesnake, good food and drink, and great company.

Gib's friend Sally, then president of Sierra Design, her parents, her long time girl friend Rachel, two of her brothers, and one young nephew were in our party. Both her father and I were World War II combat infantry veterans. Seriously wounded in the fighting ahead of the Allied breakout at St. Lô, he later recovered and became a successful surgeon. We had much in common and shared many memories over cocktails in the evenings. At one point on our trip, while riding a particularly treacherous rapid, Sally and Rachel pulled me to safety as our raft went vertical and we lost our single oarsman.

On several occasions I flew co-pilot with Gib in his Cessna – once to Seattle to look for another store location in addition to the one in San Francisco, once to Wisconsin where Karna lived, and several times to a Montana horse and cattle ranch belonging to his relatives. On the Seattle flight we flew very close to Mount St.Helen and viewed the enormous crater left following its violent eruption. Remembering that my wife and children had camped at Spirit Lake on that very mountain during our time living in Portland, and realizing that it was no longer there was quite a feeling. On that same flight, returning from Seattle, we bypassed a violent thunder and lightening storm by flying out over the Pacific and visibility was zero when we came in for an instrument landing at the Napa Airport. We only saw ground when our wheels touched the runway. Flying with Gib was always a thrill. I trusted him completely and was never afraid.

When I went to Actors Theatre in Louisville for the Humana Festival of New American Plays Gib often joined me. While Richard likes theatre, sitting through five or six full-length plays in the space of two and one-half days had no appeal for him. (Toward the end of my affair with Gib, The Humana Festival was the only time we saw each other in any given year. He had done some acting in college and once saw me playing Mr. De Pinna in *You Can't Take It With You* at my theatre club in New York.)

Another thing we had in common was our love of dogs. Border Collies. Eventually he, his former housemate in Berkeley, and his business partner in Sonoma had seven Border Collies between them. All now live on Whidbey Island in Puget Sound near Seattle and the dogs have many acres in which to run and chase Frisbees. It's now been more than seven years since I've seen any of them, but we still stay in touch..

Early in my relationship with Gib, Richard had asked that I talk to our mutual friend Molly McGreevy, a priest who was at St. Luke's at the time. Then married to the TV series actor who played the "neighbor across the fence whom you never saw", Molly had children by her first husband, was in no way judgmental, and was as gay friendly as any person could be. Richard, who has no use for organized religion, once told her, after she moved to Stamford, Connecticut, that we had lost the last true Christian in all of New York. She liked Richard immensely and the feeling between them was mutual.

When I told Molly why I had come to her, that I found myself in love with two guys at the same time, she smiled and said, "What's wrong with that?" Obviously for Molly, the answer was "Nothing."

When I told Richard, I'm afraid it didn't help much. He also asked that I speak with Dr. Gary Portadin, the psychiatrist we both had seen following his suicide attempt in 1977. Gary listened to my story – how Gib and I met, what he meant to me, that I couldn't help loving both Gib and Richard – and dismissed me after one session.

He said, "I can't help you."

I later learned from Richard that Gary felt he couldn't help because I thought I didn't have a problem. And (selfishly) as far as I was concerned, I didn't.

But dear Richard did. That spring when Gib and I returned to New York from our first trip together to Louisville for the Humana Festival I found a note from Richard saying he was leaving me.

Never had I wanted this to happen. When I called him at his brother's Southampton home to tell him that he had mail and that I wanted him to return, he did so. For a brief period we agreed that I could be with Gib whenever he was in New York, but that we would have to stay elsewhere – at Gib's hotel. When I told my daughter this, she told me it wouldn't work. And she was right.

Eventually, the distance that separated us, and my desire never to walk away from Richard, brought my sexual relationship with Gib to an end. We remain good friends, remember each other's birthday, and talk occasionally by phone. Though Richard insisted that this memoir include Gib, I have come to accept the fact that he prefers never to speak of him at all. Our bedroom walls have photos of all the Border Collies Gib ever owned. (Above my computer station are photos of my former wife, children and grandchildren, a favorite photo of Richard and me taken on one of our annual winter vacations in Saint Barth, and a single photo taken of

Gib and me during that memorable whitewater rafting trip through the Grand Canyon.)

So what is wrong with being in love with more than one person at a time? I have to agree with Mother Molly. Though I regret the pain it gave Richard. My childhood friend Lucille New was probably right. I really can be the most selfish, egotistical person.

CHAPTER EIGHTEEN: **From The Children**

JOHN PIERPONT OSTRUM
Born New Haven, Connecticut, January 11, 1950
April 3, 2005

Dear Dad,

For some time now I have struggled with your request to provide you with a written piece for inclusion in your memoirs. It is a psychologically difficult request to fulfill for I am at peace with where our father/son relationship has evolved to – and I do not want any words that I might say here to come to change or damage our relationship in any way. Getting to my plane of mental well being has been painful and reliving the past is like re-opening an old wound that one considers healed. Moreover, as a person whose life work is in the built environment, I do not trust this process of putting words to paper. The author never gets all their feelings down precisely and the reader never can interpret those written words exactly as the author intended. One might as well cast seeds into a strong wind and try to predict where the seeds will land and which ones will germinate and take root. So,…I will share my thoughts of you because you have asked, and in return I ask that you remember my analogy of words as wind blown seeds. Please do not judge me harshly if I measure short as a wordsmith – for these words are offered only in love.

Endings:

Of late, as I have witnessed with more frequency the passing of people I have known, I have begun to contemplate what I will feel when you are no longer alive. What I project I will feel is a sense of loss – despite the physical distance between us – for the reassuring presence of a loved one lost. It will only be a partial loss though – because I know I will continue to feel comforted by thoughts of your spirit – in the same way I am comforted by thoughts of Okas and Helen (and oddly, comforted also by thoughts of your grandparents even though I really only know them by their pictures). This expected feeling of loss is also reinforced by the only memory I ever have had of you crying – in a car on the way to the Bunker Hill cemetery after Okas's funeral in the spring of 1969. These positive spiritual feelings would not be possible though unless I had good memories of you and Sari (yes you and Sari – for the two of you are entwined in my mind and I can not separate you).

Beginnings:
I have very strong, vivid, pleasant memories of beginning life in Russell, Kansas (I have no memories of New Haven or Chicago). In particular I remember our house, Okas and Helen's house, the smell of their juniper bushes, their cool basement and Helen's jars of cereal, Okas's apple juice and root beer floats, linoleum countertops, food scraps tied up with string in newspaper, Okas's chess board, the town park and slippery slide, the town swimming pool, the Sunday school teacher with the missing fingers, Okas singing to me at night, Okas and Helen driving Karna and me out north of town into the hills at dusk to play peek-a-boo with the rising moon, Master the dog, dancing on the sewer manhole cover to hear it's cover ring like a steel drum, my tricycle ride to Ben Brook's grocery store, oil wells, Dango touching my face, flashes of Dango's funeral, and letting Elsie's herd of black angus cattle out of the corral the day Sari picked gooseberries. Then the

moves began in earnest and each city was an adventure with its own special memories. 99.9% of these are positive memories (Hope I got all the years correct):

Topeka ('53) – Ladybug I. and her litter of puppies. Wetting my pants at Karna's kindergarten 'show and tell' while waiting for the puppies, waiting behind the living room sofa with you for Santa Claus

St. Louis ('54) – Crying until you bought me double holstered cap guns, learning to ride Karna's 'two wheeler', my Lionel train

Dallas ('55) – Indian Guides as Big and Little White Eagle, you carving the best section of the tribal totem pole of all the dads (you carved wings), learning to climb the metal pole & ringing the bell at kindergarten, our trip to the Alamo and meeting Mr. Texas

Long Island ('56) – Williamsburg in winter on the drive from Dallas, the spooky Lincoln house with all its books, guns, attic, mysterious garden, Morris the Scotsman, skipping stones at the ocean, our trip to the Statue of Liberty

Back to Dallas ('56) – Sari and GM & the Mrs. Eddy pilgrimage, DC & Jamestown, Sari pregnant with Peter

Portland ('57) – your solo winter drive with Karna, me and Danny out to Portland, getting stuck in a snow storm in Little America, Wyoming, choking on a red life saver, getting stopped by the Oregon Highway Patrol near Multnomah Falls, our big new house in Sylvan and all the new neighborhood kids, the 'blue' Austin Healey – my favorite car ever,

Saucer the black lab and your attempt to build a dog run (that was the 1st time I remember hearing you swear – you said 'shit' over the difficulties of getting the concrete slab poured), going sledding on Mt. Hood, going camping at Scout Lake and you almost drowning, various trips to the Oregon beaches and the starfish episode, my failures at being a great baseball player in Little League, your taking Danny and me to the 'YMCA' to play paddle racket, the day you received your discharge papers from the Army reserves. (I remember being outdoors with you at the mailbox – you were overjoyed and relieved to get them.)

Seattle ('60) – another new house, helping me with my paper route on Sunday mornings and never complaining, taking me to the Athletic Club to work out on the nights you and Sari took dancing lessons, camping on the Olympic peninsula, 'Y' camp at Spirit Lake and Mt. St. Helen's, our trip to Yellowstone & Glacier National Parks, Sky Valley Ranch & the Colorado cabin, the Jaguar XKE, your chaperoning ski school and being president, my new 'Head' skis

Cleveland ('63) – Byron Jr. High and 'Harvey', Shaker Heights High & Karna's various boyfriends, the Chuck and book 'Candy' incident when you burned his college homework in the fireplace (the maddest I have ever seen you), all your civic activities, AFS, Meg, University School, Bill Warner and I being best friends, the great coming of age summer of Outward Bound / farming in Colorado / working at Sky Valley Ranch on the landscape crew / hitch hiking to Chanute, the pain and confusion of Father Tom and your lack of concern for me (at least that's what it felt like to me over the time he tried to seduce me), Bill and me talking to the U.S. Marine recruiter our senior year and you (thank god) advising me that this war was different and that you didn't recommend enlisting

St. Louis ('68) – off on my own as a college Freshman and missing home, wanting to take a year off but not wanting to be sent to Vietnam, your finding me an apartment for my Sophomore year and driving out in the fall of '69 to help me move in (a great act of kindness and trust on your part), letting Meg and me get married and helping us out with our first apartment

My Early Middle Years:
Cleveland ('72) – Meg and I in Cleveland Heights, Schafer Flynn van Dijk Dalton-Grimm Johnson, the Cleveland Museum of Art, Monie Geismer's passing away, your move to the country with Sari, Peter & Princess the horse, Minneapolis / St. Paul & Your Move to NYC/New Jersey ('75 – '82) – the beginning of the 'dark years', the great family crisis of 1977, coming apart and new beginnings, NYC full time for you & your divorce from Sari

(It is here in this time period that I think the most important changes in our father/son relationship occurred. In the course of your coming to terms with being a gay man, I felt distrustful of you – and as silly as it may sound now – a feeling that you only married and had a family because you had felt pressured by society – and consequently felt that you may have not really wanted a wife or children. Ironically, at the same moment in time, I was pleased and proud of you for becoming honest about your inner feelings so that you could stop leading a double life.

You countered my feelings of rejection toward you with expressions of sincere interest in my life, with phone calls and letters, and with Christmas and birthday contacts and visits. Gradually I came to trust you again and was able to feel love for you again. You became a better father than you ever had been when you lived with Sari and had her to rely on for 'children' events. You also became a great Grandfather as your grand children slowly arrived over the ensuing years. Thank you for persevering and not giving up. Your actions healed a painful situation that could have gone on unresolved indefinitely.)

My Late Middle Years:
So I am now at peace with where our ship has come to rest. I am truly proud of my gifted father – for all that he has accomplished in his life – his work, his civic participation, his generosity, his calligraphy, his acting abilities, his skill with learning new languages, his hospice work, his life long love of learning (and enthusiastically still learning at age 83), – and yes, his family. I love Sari, Karna, Danny and Peter – Richard too. I enjoy spending time with each of them and celebrating their individual life gifts.

There are days I wish I had accomplished even half as much as you have. My life seems very small and ordinary in comparison. I take courage from your positive role model and the zest for life you have always shown. I try to be a good husband and father and give back for the greater good of humanity through my work as an architect specializing in public work and civically to my community when possible. I especially look forward to 'retiring' so that I can have as much fun hopefully in the next phase of my life as you have had in your so called 'retirement'. Have you started Italian lessons yet?

KARNA OSTRUM HANNA
Born New Haven, Connecticut, April 13, 1948

One of the surest things I know is that each and every one of us hungers to be accepted and loved for whom we truly are. When my Dad was outed by my brother, I was thirty and pregnant with my second child. I am sure that he would have never come out on his own. But, when confronted with the truth, I felt that he was relieved to have the deception over. He flew in to see me and talk to me in person – something that I am sure was not easy. I was grateful for this gesture.

In the beginning, I was confused, sad, and angry. Suddenly, the illusion of my "perfect" family was shattered and I had to come to terms with my father in a whole new way. I was deeply concerned for my mother and very worried about my youngest brother who was a freshman in college. Being the only daughter, I empathized a great deal with my Mom.

All divorces are painful, but ones that involve a gay spouse are far more complicated. Knowing that my Dad still loved my Mom was in some ways a bitter pill to swallow. Their continuing love for each other, in spite of their inability to continue on with their marriage, has made it possible in later years to still operate together within the context of the whole family in a loving way. I give so much credit to my Mom for her ability to forgive and move on and to my Dad's partner to share Dad with all of us in complex family settings. I know it has not been easy for either one. It means a lot to me that we can all be together and enjoy our time with each other.

Today, at least in larger cities, there are support groups to help the families of gays and lesbians.

Twenty-seven years ago I know my mother, my brothers and I didn't really know where to turn to except each other, our spouses, and girlfriends, and our own private prayers. Over the years, I have shared this part of my life with close friends who have been very supportive and understanding, not just of me, but of my entire family.

One of the hardest things to deal with was explaining the situation to our children. We decided that we would wait for our kids to give us clues that they were ready to be told and in their own sweet ways they asked the right questions and were comfortable with the answer – because they loved their Grandfather whom they had come to know as a caring, loving man and because we had raised them to be tolerant and respectful of all people. This was the foundation of their relationship and allowed the revelation of their Grandfather's sexual orientation to be a sidebar.

Of course, the irony will always be that if Dad hadn't married and remained in the closet all of those years, none of us kids, grandchildren, and great grandchildren would be here today. And if Dad hadn't married, he would never have experienced the deep joys of being a husband, parent and grandparent.

There is a part of me that will always be sad that my parents are not together. This I think is probably a feeling that all children of divorce have, no matter what age they are or what was the cause of the dissolution of the marriage. But I know deep in my heart that it is better to have two separated parents that love me, who respect themselves because they are not living a lie – either with each other or with themselves. In the end, we have all learned greater lessons of tolerance and acceptance. We love each other, just as we are, and what greater gift can we give to each other?

Karna Ostrum Hanna
December 30, 2004

* * *

Prior to receiving the above contribution from my daughter we exchanged the following correspondence following our annual family reunion at Thanksgiving.

Dear Dad,
December 1,2004
After you left we all had a lot of discussion about the possible publication of your memoirs. I'm writing on behalf of all of us. We think it's great that you're writing your life story, but are concerned in a variety of different ways about having what seems very private – out there for everyone to read.

I'm not sure you are aware that just by doing a personal name search on 'Google' on the Internet brings up even the most obscure publications or websites where you are mentioned. We may be overly sensitive here, but this can potentially be a serious matter.

Just as you have been careful about whom you have shared knowledge about your sexual orientation, so have we. You are now in a safe environment for your story to be told. You need to understand that everyone in the family is not. I know that this is your life, and it is your right to say what you want, but like most things in life, it's complicated.

It would help all of us if you could share with us who the intended audience of the book is. This would be helpful to understand your intentions and to help John, Danny, Peter, and me to write our reflections. It would also be very helpful if we could read what you have written. If this book is published, it will affect our lives too. The last thing you want to do is to create ill will within the family. We've worked too hard over the years to build good relations.

What you are asking us children to write can only have meaning if it is honest and not superficial. Honesty can be painful – both for us to relive and write about, and perhaps for you to read. It's quite possible that after you see what we've written you may decide that you do not want to include our comments. I don't mean to imply that what we might write will be all or mostly negative.

Perhaps we're all being overly concerned, but please try to look at things from our perspectives – including our spouses and children, and Mom and Richard, too. This whole project may turn out to be absolutely wonderful, but at this point we need to be convinced. Including us more in the process of what you are writing will help. We are eager to see what you have written and learn more about your life history, feelings and observations. You have lived an amazing life.

I'm sending this in writing because I thought it would be the best way to say what needed to be communicated. All of the boys have a copy of this letter. You need to know that we love you dearly and know that you will want to do what's best for everyone. Please give any of us a call to talk about things further.
Love, Karna

[Handwritten in margin: Dad – It was so good to see you at Thanksgiving. I had a good trip back arriving in Madison just about on time. Hope the Miniature Show has a successful opening. – L. K.]

During our time together at Thanksgiving I had made a point of thanking Danny for his contribution to my memoir and had reminded the other three children that I was still awaiting theirs. The above letter from Karna surprised me. I discussed with Richard how best to respond and after a couple of drafts, ended up sending Karna the following response, dated December 6, 2004, with copies to each of the boys.

> Dear Karna,
> Your letter about my memoir writing has saddened me more that I can put in words.
>
> To learn now that you have withheld from others the truth about your father's sexuality for whatever reasons is a great disappointment. Between the lines of your letter I sense an unacknowledged homophobia that is unfortunately present in much of society.
>
> Several years ago in New York you read the short Hunter College essay I had written for my Advanced Expository Writing class entitled 'Outed By My Children'. I didn't sense that it offended you. To think now that I must share my ongoing efforts to finish this project and that you may want to censure it is not something I feel right in doing.
>
> Long ago I learned from my dear friend in Cleveland that his older brother had committed suicide in California because he was gay and couldn't go on living because of it. Should my memoirs save just one young person's life I would feel it worth the effort. Originally I started writing my life history in

response to your brother John's request. 'After you're gone,' he had said, 'we won't have you around to answer questions.' Often I have wished that Okas had written about his life. Anyway as time passed I came to believe that an honest account – and I emphasize honest, showing how our wonderful family dealt with an admittedly painful crisis in all our lives might help heterosexuals to accept the minority of us who are gay and more importantly to help young gays to accept themselves.

It now seems not such a great idea that each of my children write a brief addendum telling what it was like for them to have a gay father. Dear Danny's writing, already received, touched me deeply and will always be treasured. I no longer ask that the others of you send anything.

Meanwhile, sensing that time will eventually run out, I get up most mornings, shower, shave, dress and head for a small French restaurant on Bleecker Street to have a cup of coffee and write. By the time we return mid February from St.Barth's my goal is to finish. Publication, if ever, is far away. As my friend Michael Korda says in his attached letter of rejection from Simon & Schuster, 'this is a book that is of great importance to you, and of real merit and substance, where the chief satisfaction may be in having written it.'
Much love always,
Dad

The above letter prompted telephone conversations with each of the children and in my December 15th email to Karna thanking her for the great photos she'd taken at Thanksgiving I wrote the following.

It has been wonderful to talk with each of you children about my own memoir project. As we

discussed by phone, I'm truly sorry for my over-reaction and hope you'll forgive me. I have gone back to writing, but am finding 'The Cleveland Years' chapter most difficult. The world was then, like now, in great turmoil ... [not to mention] all the many civic activities I got trapped in. Whew! And at the same time mostly wonderful and momentous events happening in our family... WOW! Enough for now. Can't wait for Betsy's visit next week.
Love, Dad"

On December 30, 2004, Karna wrote the following email to which she attached her contribution (see above).

Dear Dad –
Please find attached my reflections. I wanted you to have them, whatever you decide to do with them. I am sorry there has been so much anguish and misunderstanding over your memoirs, but sharing our feelings in a respectful way is good. I know that I/we have made Richard very angry because he has really been short with me on the phone. I know he is going through a very hard time with his parents right now and surely did not appreciate us upsetting you. Tell him I am sorry, or I will tell him directly if you think that would be better. I do not want to feel unwelcome in your home.
I hope we can all move on with greater appreciation for each other's point of view. Have a great birthday party. I'm sorry that none of us can make it this year. Betsy will be back in NYC before you leave for St. Barth's so it will be good to have her with you again. Thanks for looking after her.
Much love,
Karna
PS I'm very excited about becoming a Grandma and hope you are looking forward to your next great-

grandchild. Brid and Jason are thrilled to say the least.

PETER GARDNER OSTRUM
Born Dallas, Texas, November 1, 1957

Reflecting and trying to understand one's past, one's youth, can be difficult at best. While growing up in a privileged upper middle class community, it seemed to me that our family reflected all that was admired in the baby boom generation. Our family had talent (academic as well as athletic), a social conscience and a strong family bond. The qualities expressed by the members of my family were beacons of encouragement and hope to others and like moths drawn to light, so too were many people drawn to our family's inner circle. On the outside looking in, it appeared that we had everything, success but both humility and compassion to temper conceit. Other families had problems but not ours. In my mind we seemed to be on a stable pedestal from which we could not fall.

During my high school years, cracks in the family's foundation began to materialize. As my parent's relationship began to deteriorate, we all knew in our hearts that something was amiss. Putting the pieces of the puzzle together, it was clear that Dean had multiple issues that needed to be discussed and dealt with. My observation of this situation led me to believe that he had to acknowledge and accept who Dean Ostrum really was. In a sense, my father was outed by his own family. It was time to take off the protective mask of a wife and family and be truly honest despite the criticism and cynicism of many.

Dean's sexuality and its impact on my parent's relationship consumed our family's energy. Their marriage was like the Titanic, the band played on for a while but everyone knew that they were sinking fast. Once the divorce was finalized, it took years for damaged relationships to slowly heal. In retrospect, I blame no one for the situation in which we found ourselves. Those were simply the cards that we were dealt. It's often been said, the game of life is not so much in holding a good hand as playing a poor hand well.

Currently, my focus at 47 years of age is my own family. Each generation should improve. Right? So how do I avoid the pitfalls that my parents made? Be honest with yourself, be aware of one's limitations but don't be afraid to push through them and experience failure. It's ironic, but if coming out of the closet and being open had been an option for Dean back in the 30's and 40's, I probably wouldn't be writing this letter.

The dilemma of having a gay father is a non-issue at this point in my life. Expression of feelings, tolerance of others that are different and the ability to forgive are true hallmarks of a person's moral character regardless of their sexuality. As a parent, my mantra to my children is: be honest, be kind to each other and be willing to make the sacrifices necessary to follow your dreams. Be confident, yet humble.

The relationship with my father continues to change and evolve. That's what makes Dean so special to so many people. He isn't content to sit idle in the audience, but better yet, he is on stage crafting his talent for all of us to admire. As he once told me, you're never too young to teach and never too old to learn.

In closing, it may be best to remember that our happiness has little to do with material wealth and status. And as Charlie Bucket knew, happiness has everything to do with what's in your heart. As I parent my children, I continue to gain the utmost respect for my parents and their ability to raise a family. It's just not that easy at times. Despite the challenges our family faced, Dean will always be our loved, respected and honored father.

Here follows a December 1999 letter Peter wrote to Sari and me, some days after what became an annual family Thanksgiving gathering that, of course, includes Richard.

> Dear Mom and Dad,
> We just got our pictures back and they look super. Of course it was hard to get everybody looking their best all at once, but for the most part we all look happy and healthy, ready for the new millennium. Retta and I are going to use one of the prints (with the Woodcliff Christmas tree) to include in our Christmas cards this year.
>
> I apologize for not speaking during the toasts prior to dinner on Thursday evening. I wanted to make it special but by the time my thoughts were collected and organized the moment had passed. What I wanted to say to all the family and friends gathered was how proud I was of you two. And how honored I was to be your son and my kids to be your grandchildren. That we could all come together after so many years and so many miles to celebrate a true thanksgiving. It speaks volumes about the values and morals that you've instilled in your children.
>
> As I traveled home from Boston the week before I thought how different my life was from my fellow 'Wonka' companions. It seemed they all had troubled or difficult childhoods which in most cases led to stormy adult relationships. Fortunately I was lucky to have unique parents who provided clear and constant mentoring. I realize only now how fortunate one is to have loving parents. From my work on the school board I've discovered that many parents just don't care or can't be bothered with their kids' problems.
>
> Nobody knows how truly difficult it is to 'parent well' until they've had kids of their own. Well, I'm in

the trenches now and believe me it's the hardest job I've ever had. I can only hope that I'm half as successful as you two were. As proud as I am of my own family, my siblings and their families, both of you should be beaming. You allowed each of your children to follow their own path without undue criticism or skepticism. We always knew that we could always come home. And we did.

Our family is truly blessed this holiday season.
That is what I wanted to say.
Love, Peter

Here follows the email I sent Peter in response.
Subj: Your great letter!
Date: 99-12-22 21:09:17EST

Dear Peter,
Please know how much your great letter to your 'Mom and Dad' has meant to me. You needn't apologize for not making a toast at Thanksgiving. It was just a wonderful time we all had together. After Sari started to choke up when she said our family prayer, I felt it would help if I stood up and asked us all to join hands and really sound out with our 'Praise God from whom all blessings flow!' It was a pretty emotional
event in many ways. You were right to postpone your thoughts until now.

If I have been a good parent it's primarily because all four of you kids have been such great children. All of you are hardworking, loving, free from drugs, and even free from smoking tobacco. Most importantly we've all also followed Grandma Helen and Okas's great example of not judging others and being free from prejudice – racial, religious, and sexual as well.

My parents meant so much to me and I think of both of them often and with the fondest of memories.

As for you and Retta now being in the trenches of parenthood, I'm confident all will go equally well for you because of the kind of parents you are. No one knows what temptations of all kinds lie in store for our children, but I'm certain Leif and Helenka will continue to bless your lives. My only regret in growing older and knowing that someday I won't be here is the knowledge that I won't be living to see what all you and the grandchildren will do in their lives.

Thanks from the bottom of my heart for your thoughtful and loving letter. I still keep and treasure the one you wrote when you first faced up to your father's being gay. It meant everything to me then and still does. And this latest letter is equally important to me.

Have a wonderful Christmas and a truly Blessed New Year.
Love, Dad

DANIEL GROSS OSTRUM
Born Russell, Kansas, May 7, 1953

It was big money to me. Two cents for every weed I pulled. My Dad said he would pay me two cents for every weed I pulled on the large flowerbed that overlooked our home in Bellevue, Washington. I never got rich as a kid, but today when I am weeding my own gardens I think of that story – always with a smile.

When I was growing up my friends would tell me that my Dad was the coolest. He never lost his temper and he was nice and friendly unlike all the other dads. I felt that way myself. He would often times take me to the YMCA and we would play racquetball together and introduce me to his friends in the locker room. In fact he seemed to know everybody.

When my Dad was Vice President of Ohio Bell Telephone Company he would take me to downtown Cleveland to show me his office and would introduce me to the elevator operator and the security guard by their first names. It made them feel good that he always talked with them, and included them. Dad has the ability and the confidence to strike up a conversation with a complete stranger and put them at ease. He makes everyone feel good and makes them feel his equal.

Growing up I never knew my Dad was gay. I was twenty-three years old and married when the family found out.

One time part of the family was visiting my Dad who had an apartment in Greenwich Village. We were walking down Bleecker Street in the village and I saw for the first time two young men walking and talking together holding hands. I immediately mentioned something about what I had seen and probably even pointed at them. My Dad became quite agitated and upset with me. He said something like "until you have walked in their shoes you don't have a right to make fun of anybody." He was probably right, but I had never seen two men holding hands before.

Since I was unaware that my Dad was gay growing up I don't think it affected me one way or the other. Today, knowing my father is gay certainly has made me more tolerant of every individual's situation. I really think it has rounded me to accept all people and their orientations.

There have always been gay people. There will always be gay people. It's part of life and will always be part of life. Young generations today accept this fact of life – and so have I. I love my Dad.

Love, Danny

I would like to add an important day of my life that I will always remember.

When my parents were still married, one summer day when I was home from college painting the horse barn, the three of us were talking around the breakfast table. I can remember saying that I really wasn't sure what I wanted to do in college, let alone the rest of my life.

My Dad said that I could stay with them as long as I would like, and that I always would have a place with them! Deep down I needed that. Not that I would take them up on it. But it was just knowing I had a back up – if things didn't work out. To this day my parents have always been there for me. They are so to speak still my safety net.

P.S. My wife Jackie and I have told our children, now grown, the same story. And it's a true story.
Love, Danny
Here follows a letter from Danny to me that was written ten years before the above.

> 1-3-94
> Dear Dad,
> Enclosed you will find the other review Sari was mentioned in. Maybe next year they will get to perform in front of the Rochester RPO (Philharmonic). Wouldn't that be great!
>
> How was your party on your birthday? The reason I was rather quiet while talking with you on the phone was because I was trying to also carry on a conversation at the same time with Sari. She finally popped
> the question about "is Grandpa Dean gay". I answered yes and she said "does Cody [her older

brother] know?" I said I think so but he has never asked. I went skating with her later in the afternoon. She, I think knew but was a little hesitant to bring it up. I did tell her please ask me anything you ever want to know. She did ask why Grandpa Dean married Grandma Sari. I said because he loves her. And if they didn't get married
they wouldn't have had me – and then I wouldn't have married mom – and then we could not have had you or Cody, and she nodded. She probably is still thinking. I don't think it was any big news to her. Have to get to work.
Love, Danny

CHAPTER NINETEEN: Memories Of Death

What happens when you die?

Well, first they have to get rid of your body. Next, there may or may not be some kind of funeral or memorial service. You're now only memories, for good or for bad, and only then when someone still living has the time to think about you. As William Hazlitt once said, "There was a time when we were not: this gives us no concern – why then should it trouble us that a time will come when we shall cease to be?"

On the other hand, is there really some sort of something after death? Or is the whole exercise just wishful thinking?

Following retirement in 1985, I applied for and was accepted in a 4-month class for hospice volunteers at St. Vincent's Hospital and Medical Center in New York City. By that time I had had several acquaintances die of AIDS and I wanted to find some way I might help in the crisis. One night during my class's final week of training, our instructor pointed out that a dying patient occasionally asks the question "What do you think will happen when I die?" We should be prepared, she told us, to answer truthfully for ourselves, honesty being paramount.

Divided into groups of five, we then shared our responses. The most adamant among us was a beautiful young painter who worked at the Metropolitan Museum of Art. She was a born-again Christian with no doubts whatsoever. Jesus himself would be there to take her into his arms and welcome her to Heaven. Another, a striking black woman who was a horticulturist and made her living healing sick plants, believed strongly in reincarnation. Two, including myself, were agnostics, my fellow traveler being a recent graduate of Oberlin College. She had been admitted to the Harvard Medical School for the following fall. The fifth and last to speak was a gentle appearing, middle-aged nun wearing simple street clothes. A tiny gold cross hung around her pale throat. She had endeared herself to many throughout our weeks together by her judicious comments and joyous demeanor.

"What will happen when I die?" Sister Mary Ellen murmured softly, repeating the question. "Frankly, I don't know."

There was silence. We were amazed. Having just confessed my agnosticism, I personally felt a little smug.

Then suddenly, having paused for breath, Sister continued in a stronger voice. "But I'm certain of two things – there will be something more, and it will be very good."

I have always been curious about death, which is one of the other reasons I wanted to do hospice work. Death was the subject of one of my earliest childhood memories and subsequent deaths of immediate family members are easy for me to recall.

One cold winter night when I was four years old, my Uncle Francis took me in his arms and carried me into the front room of my paternal grandmother's tiny white frame house in the small farming community of Bunker Hill, to see her lying very still in a casket.

She was wearing a dress, rather fancy, undoubtedly new store-bought, wholly unlike the large, faded, loose-fitting ones I had always seen her in. I thought how different she looked in this funny box full of lavender ruffles, compared with the last time I had seen her – sitting on a kitchen stool peeling potatoes from her garden and wearing a large, soiled apron tied around her round and stocky frame.

No one spoke. She didn't move or smile. We all just looked. I could smell carnations and a strange pungent, yet sweet, odor of what I much later learned was embalming fluid. It was creepy, and although I wasn't frightened, it felt good to leave that room.

When I was fourteen, my maternal grandfather, whom we called Papa, died suddenly one unbearably hot summer's day of a heart attack. The country was in the midst of the Great Depression and Kansas was in the midst of those terrible dust bowl years. It happened while he was hanging up wet clothes for my grandmother in the back yard of their gingerbread-like, many-porched beige house in that same town. When he didn't return from the oppressive heat, my tiny, frail grandmother went out to find his body lying peacefully in the brown, sun-parched buffalo grass beneath her clothesline.

Sudden death is shocking, but for my grandmother, it was catastrophic. That very night she came to live with my family and never left – my father graciously insisting that her home was now with us.

Though Papa's funeral was held in his old limestone Lutheran church in Bunker Hill, his body lay in state for two days in our front parlor. This gave me a chance to view his remains at close range, which I surreptitiously did one night after everyone else had gone to bed. His casket had grey ruffles, more appropriate, I thought, for a man. Carefully I touched his forehead. It wasn't ice cold, but it certainly wasn't warm like mine. Then I felt his rigid left hand, clasped piously with the other on his chest. He was wearing his dark gray suit and a vest with gold chain and large pocket watch. I can still remember how he used to take it out to wind every day when he heard the Union Pacific train whistle. He always remarked to my grandmother about the punctuality, or lack thereof, of their principal means of long-distance travel in those early days.

When my mother's mother, whom we called Dango, died at ninety-one in her bedroom at my parents' home, she was blind. Almost to the end of her life she had faithfully continued to dry the supper dishes which my mother washed by hand every evening. And she loved to run her gnarled, bony fingers through the fine, blond hair of our second child, a little boy she had never seen.

By this time, Russell, had a real funeral home run by a real funeral director, no longer just the furniture man doubling in the role of undertaker on the side. Since Papa's congregation had merged with the Methodists and since his old stone church was now the tiny community's historical museum, Dango's service was held in the funeral home with only family and a few close friends in attendance. She was buried beside Papa in the Bunker Hill cemetery – a peaceful, well-kept square of ground on a hill covered with prairie grass and drought-resisting old juniper trees.

My father died at eighty-four within hours of suffering a heart attack while walking from the post office to his second floor office. (He was still practicing law more than a year after his announced retirement.) My mother was blessed with a century of good health, and a sound mind to the very end. After my father's death she lived quietly alone in the house I grew up in until some months after reaching 100, when she suffered a crippling stroke. Thereafter she was cared for in the local hospital, regaining the ability to speak, her delightful sense of humor, and her love of family visits. In accordance with her wishes, she received no special life support beyond loving care from the nurses. Gradually refusing nourishment, she slowly died of starvation, but with no sign of pain.

Aside from those of my family, deaths I witnessed during war are among my most vivid memories. In my early twenties, I spent eight long months in combat in Europe as an armored infantry officer in World War II. The gruesome indignity of death in war is beyond belief unless you've been there. In France I carried a blown-off leg, severed by shrapnel at the hip, ten yards back to the now dead body it had seconds earlier been attached to. In Holland I picked up the shattered body of a young boy hit by enemy mortar fire while taking a break in a barn; I saw his guts and private parts, warm and steaming in the bitter cold, spill out on the floor as I placed his lifeless body on a stretcher.

During the Battle of the Bulge I made a hurried visit to a tented army field hospital near the frontlines in Belgium. The friend I went to see was still alive in the intensive care tent where he lay on an army cot, oxygen tubes in his nostrils and IV tubes in his arms. As I left he had tears in his eyes. He was unable to speak, but pleased that I had come. Rushing to my jeep to return to the front, I noticed a huge canvas-covered army truck parked nearby. The rear flaps were open exposing layer upon layer of naked cadavers, stacked to the ceiling like a neat pile of cordwood. In the pile near the bottom I recognized the stiffened body of an infantry officer friend from my battalion, wounded and evacuated to that field hospital a few days before.

Proper funerals for these men would come months later, but the exigencies of war apparently precluded even the simple dignity of a mattress cover to enshroud their remains.

Some time ago I found a book entitled First Cut – *A Season in the Human Anatomy Lab* by Albert Howard Carter III. It is an account of a semester the author spent watching first-year medical students at Emory University in Atlanta dissect their cadavers. At page 286, the following appears. "On Thursday, their 'joint' exam will finish the anatomy course entirely... Some students are planning on leaving Friday. The new paths open up and out. As for the cadavers, their path will go like this: in the next two days, their remains go to the basement for temporary storage on trays. Then, in sets of two, they travel to the crematory, a few miles away. I learn this from Jim Cooper, the embalmer, who will work on these final dispositions. Jim says the crematorium can't handle more than a few bodies at a time, since the bodies are burned individually to keep the ashes separate. (It takes two or three hours to burn a body and cool the ashes.) "Besides, we don't stack them," he says. "That's not right."

In the past dozen years I have attended numerous memorial services for people who died of AIDS. Following the hospice training described earlier, I spent seven years caring for mostly young patients who later died in this horrific plague. After periods of deep anger at their predicament, most seemed to accept their approaching death with a calm at which I marveled. As in war, the ravages wreaked on a young body from AIDS can be appalling.

Without exception, I came to care deeply for every one of my patients. Though their bodies were often so wasted that even friends failed to recognize them, the wonderful human being was still somewhere inside, up to the very instant that death took its toll. How could it be true that there wasn't some sort of something after these soon-to-be-useless bodies ceased physical functioning?

None of my patients ever asked me the question about what would happen when they died. Then early one June morning several years ago, a young man with AIDS came for breakfast on our terrace and to pick up some calligraphy I had done for the restaurant where he worked. Once a Greek Adonis with shiny-black, curly hair and sparkling, dark eyes, Nino was now frail and emaciated. It was a clear, sunny day; the flowers, trees, and shrubs were especially beautiful, having been washed by a shower the previous night.

After he had finished his coffee and was preparing to leave, his eyes filled with tears and he suddenly said, "I'm so afraid, Dean." Taking him into my arms, I hugged him as he sobbed. Then he added, "I'm so afraid that tomorrow I won't be here."

At that moment in my life I finally found the courage to say it, to voice for Nino what I'd come to believe. "It's true," I found myself telling him, "tomorrow you may not be here; but it's also true, Nino, that tomorrow you will be somewhere."

"Do you really believe that?" he asked, incredulous.

"Yes, I do," I replied.

As his tears ceased to flow and a smile came over his angelic face, I told him the story of Sister Mary Ellen and that night at hospice training years earlier. Like myself, Nino seemed to find great comfort in Mary Ellen's firm conviction that there would be something tomorrow, and that it would be something very good.

Nino died the following week.

Twenty-plus years later, I attended the wedding of my oldest grandson Jason and his Irish bride Brid in the little Catholic church where she was baptized, in County Limerick.

At the ceremony only Catholics in attendance were served the host and wine during Communion. (This was not surprising to me since I had had a similar experience several years earlier when I attended the wedding of one of Richard's female cousins on Long Island. At the reception afterward I was introduced to the young Catholic priest, a brother of the groom, and his gay partner. When in our conversation the priest learned that I was an Episcopalian, he informed me that he would have refused me the host at the mass had he known I was not Catholic.)

At the wedding of Jason and Brid, Jason, too, was not welcome at the Lord's table and was told beforehand that he should not open his hands to receive the host. (Is it any wonder that our world is torn with war and killings? More often than not over religious differences.) Brid had asked me to read the First Lesson and I had happily accepted. The reading was the famous one on Love from Second Corinthians. It concludes with the sentence, "Love does not come to an end." The Second Reading, given by Brid's youngest sister, embodies the statement "God is Love."

With these two readings I was at peace, despite my disappointment that the Catholic Church refused to embrace all of us at the Lord's table in celebration of the marriage of dear Jason and Brid.

I will never forget how Sister Patrice welcomed all volunteers to the Saint Vincent's Hospital hospice program – whether they were Catholic, Protestant, Buddhist, Muslim, born-again Christians, agnostic or atheist. Hopefully religious hypocrisy will one day end and we will accept all human beings as worthy of respect.

APPENDICES

APPENDIX #L In the district court of Russell, Kansas
In the Matter }
of the } Case No. 10,711
Memorial to OSCAR OSTRUM }
Proceedings In Memory of Oscar Ostrum
MAY IT PLEASE THE COURT:

We are assembled this morning to pay our respects and tribute to our departed colleague, Oscar Ostrum. Although some record of his service appears throughout the files of this court, it is only fitting and proper that we pause on this occasion to recognize his contributions.

Oscar Ostrum was a native of Russell County. He was born in northwest Russell County November 26, 1884. He passed on to his reward on April 24, 1969, at the age of 84 years. His early education was in the Bunker Hill Schools. His college education was at Bethany College in Lindsborg, Kansas, from which he received his A. B. Degree in 1904. He was admitted to the practice of law in the State and Federal Courts in 1915 and to the United States Supreme Court in 1938. He signed the Registry of Attorneys in this court on June 24, 1915. He was the official court reporter of the 23rd Judicial District from 1907 to 1916. He served as County Attorney and City Attorney and on the City Council and the Board of Education. He was an active abstracter from 1924 and was President of Russell County Abstracting, Inc. at the date of his death. From January, 1952 to January, 1953 he served as President of our own Russell County Bar Association. He was a member of the American Bar Association and of the Kansas Bar Association, and from the latter was awarded a 50 year certificate in 1965. He was an active member of the Trinity Methodist Church, having served on its Board of Trustees and as Superintendent of the Sunday School. He was a member of the Bunker Hill Masonic Lodge and Isis Shrine Temple. In 1967 he was awarded the Alumni Award of Merit by the Bethany College Alumni Association. He was a

Charter member and a former President of the Russell Rotary Club. He is survived by his wife Helen Gross Ostrum, to whom he was married on November 26, 1914, their two sons, Dean G. and Wilbur G., both of whom are lawyers, and by seven grandchildren. But this listing of vital statistics is but skeletal evidence of the accomplishments of our late departed colleague. His training and education to be admitted to the bar was not in the organized curriculum of a law school, but in the more difficult manner of reading the law in a lawyer's office. His records and accomplishments however, are shining examples of hat recognized fact, that there were great lawyers long before there were law schools. He would have been the first to confess that a lawyer's education is never completed, and his office was replete with evidence that he never stopped his educational process. In addition to a highly adequate law library, he had books on many subjects, all of which bear evidence of his study of them. In his early life as a lawyer, he practiced with L. B. Beardsley. In later years he practiced in partnership with his son, Dean G. Ostrum, and still later with J. Eugene Balloun, now of Great Bend, Kansas. But for the most part, he served in the sometime solitary confines of a sole practitioner of the law. His work as a lawyer was truly that of general practitioner. His practice covered every field of the law in which a Mid-Western lawyer might become engaged. He was equally at home in trial courts, the State Supreme Court and on one occasion in the United States Supreme Court. But his work in the courts, while perhaps the more glamorous and the best-recorded evidence of his service as a lawyer, was possibly not his greatest contribution in the service of his clients. It is impossible to estimate the number of people, or their problems, whom he consulted and advised, or for whom he drafted wills, conveyances, contracts, or any of a myriad of documents. His services were equally available to the poor and the affluent, and he exhibited the same devotion of duty in protecting the anonymity of the fallen angel as in handling a multi-million dollar lawsuit. His relationship with other lawyers was exemplary. He was always available for consultation by a young lawyer, and though his adversary knew that he must be well prepared when Oscar was on the other side, he also knew that Oscar Ostrum would never assert any unfair advantage. It has been said that a man best serves God by serving other men. Oscar Ostrum must have been a disciple of that maxim. His records and accomplishments are at one and the same time a sterling example and a rich heritage to the people of Russell County in general and to the Russell County Bar in particular.

Submitted this 26th day of May, 1969.

RUSSELL COUNTY BAR
ASSOCIATION
Rex Culley, President

APPENDIX #2

PRESIDENT'S PAGE Spring 1985 D.C. Bar Magazine
"District Lawyer" page 6

A CONTENT MAN

By Marna S. Tucker

I don't know Dean Ostrum. I've never met him. But he's on my short list of heroes. I don't know what he looks like, but I picture him as a man very much in the corporate mainstream. After all, he spent 31 years working for Ma Bell before he retired as vice president and general counsel of the Ohio Bell Telephone Company. I'm sure he wore three-piece suits, played a lot of golf and had season tickets to the theatre. There is something slightly different about him. I'll bet he wore a plaid bow-tie and a rakish hat with that three-piece suit. And I know that he's not at all satisfied with stare decisis. His name came up in casual conversation a few months ago. And then again. I've since learned a little about him, and I'd like to know more. I'd like to find out what he's made of, because he's done in his professional life what I want to do in mine. He's a man of vision who has made a critical difference in the lives of a number of members of the District of Columbia Bar, and through them, to our profession. Many of us, once we get a few years under our belt, find ourselves giving a helping hand to young lawyers, newly out of school. But not many of us will be able to claim a Court of Appeals Chief judge, a Hogan & Hartson partner, or a D.C. Bar president-elect. Dean Ostrum can claim all three. And he might have been able to add a Secretary of the Army had it not been Cleveland.

What makes Ostrum so special is not the keen scouting eye, but the fact that the lawyers he recruited over twenty years ago, before Title VII, before fair housing and public accommodations, were black.

The story goes that in the early 1960's, ATT decided to hire more minority employees. Ostrum was one of a very few senior executives who took the message to heart. He began to recruit the best black lawyers he could find for his staff. No one told Ostrum what to do or how to do it. There were no affirmative action guidelines, no "outreach programs," no convention lists for "qualified black lawyers." He did it because it was right, and because it was the smart thing to do. Ostrum first contacted his Yale Law School classmate, U.S. District Judge Leon Higginbotham in Philadelphia.

Judge Higginbotham introduced him to several black lawyers and judges in Philadelphia who then introduced him to several Washington lawyers. He offered positions to several lawyers whose names will ring a bell to you. Young William Pryor was the first lawyer he hired in Washington and spirited away to Cleveland. Frederick Abramson could not be persuaded to leave Washington, but Ostrum didn't want to miss that catch, so he arranged a position for him at ATT Longlines. Vincent Cohen moved to Cleveland to work with Ostrum. And several other minority lawyers joined his small staff. Cliff Alexander got away. Cleveland, after all, is not paradise. Ostrum claims that it was easy to find excellent black lawyers, even 20 years ago when minority lawyers were in shorter supply. His major problem was to lure them to Cleveland from Washington, D.C. And once the lawyers worked for him in Ohio, he found he had trouble keeping them on his staff. "My lawyers opened the eyes of the elite bar in Cleveland who saw them in action—in the courtroom—in professional civic activities," Ostrum told me. The large law firms started hiring his lawyers away from him. They asked for the "list" compiled from his trips to Washington and Philadelphia. In effect he became a talent scout for the local bar. Eventually, Washington too lured back some of the lawyers he brought out to Cleveland. They became some of the stars in our legal community. Pryor, Cohen and Abramson have made it by any standard. Each of them will tell you that their futures were cast by Ostrum's efforts. And we of the D.C. Bar, of course, are the beneficiaries of all of this legal talent. Ostrum is content.

Here it is twenty years later, with excellent minority lawyers all across the country, and I read disheartening statistics like those in a 1983 study by the National Association for Law Placement. Of 296 firms in 12 cities only 2.7 per cent reported having minority lawyers in their offices. The percentage of blacks in many of these firms has declined over the last ten years even though the number of black graduates from the finest law schools in the country has grown.

From 1963 to 1973 substantial progress was made for black lawyers, but the moral pressure of the civil rights movement has faded. Progress has essentially stopped. In the District of Columbia, we still have only a handful of minority partners in major law firms. We fare better than New York City which has had six black partners in all its major law firms. But it is hardly a horse race. And there is a high turnover of black lawyers in law firms. Some ascribe the high turnover to continuing discrimination in firms—minority leaders leave when they are not assigned major clients and know they aren't going to make partner. Some complain that blacks aren't being taken in the subtle acculturation process of a law firm. The low numbers and high turnover are puzzling problems. This state of affairs doesn't make sense to me. It seems so obvious that there are sound business reasons for law firms aggressively to hire and promote minority lawyers. More black lawyers are getting a crack at jobs in

D.C.'s law departments and minority practitioners are logical choices to handle significant city business.

But more than sound business reasons requires us to change this situation. It is ironic that the legal profession, which spearheaded an extraordinary legal and social revolution in our country, has been so woefully lax in putting our own house in order.

The profession can prosper only by broadening its diversity of lawyers. Competence demands sensitivity to our clients and their interests. Our clients are multi-racial and multi-cultural. Our system of justice is only as strong as the confidence it commands from all persons in our society. We need more Dean Ostrums in our ranks to take positive measures to hire and promote all minorities and women. It's not difficult to do—it's only difficult to decide to do. Neutrality is not good enough to combat discrimination. The status quo is short-sighted for our profession. There are a lot of potential chief judges and bar presidents out there. It is up to us to find them.

APPENDIX #3
CLEVELAND PLAIN DEALER
August 8, 1968
ADELE Z. SILVER
54 GIVE A BOOST TO 35,000

The slings and arrows that have recently been aimed at the Mayor's Council on Youth Opportunity, which operates under Cleveland NOW! could, through public misunderstanding and distrust, jeopardize the intelligent and hopeful plans— to say nothing of the money—that went into the Council's programs. Like a lot of other public committees, the Mayor's Council is attacked from one side as "a bunch of soft headed do-gooders" and from the other as "fat cat Establishment types." FIFTY FOUR CITIZENS are members of the Council. Some of them do indeed represent the traditional wealth and power of the community—industrialists, managers, lawyers, a few of whom belong to restricted clubs or firms with narrow hiring policies. Another segment of the membership comprises the old and new groups representing the part of the community without money or influence—welfare agencies, religious groups, neighborhood associations. Ten members are young persons, all under 21, who represent that section of the community the Council serves. Together, these very different citizens chose 36 projects to try to meet the needs of as many and as varied groups of youngsters as there are in the city. Those three dozen programs are costing $750,000, none of it federal, state or city money. By far the largest chunk is going to the Summer Arts Festival: $225,000. Anybody who could have gone with me over to Lincoln Park, on the Near West Side, to see youngsters performing Eastern European folk dances and an audience mellow with memories, wouldn't begrudge the expenditures for these festival nights that have brightened life all around town. The next biggest cut went to the Welfare Federation, the Y's and the Scouts, for camperships, about $150,000 all told. By the end of summer, between 4,000 and 4,500 street-wise youngsters will have had a sniff of fresh country air. Nearly $6,000 went to the Spanish-American Committee for a job program for Puerto Rican youth. $15,000 went to the Police Athletic League to keep its centers open later at night. Pride, Inc., got $40,000 to employ adults to work with kids on both sides of town. $4,000 went to John Carroll University for a college prep course for "academically capable" high school students. On and on the list goes, a reflection of the diversity of the city's people and their hopes.

THERE'S A GOOD DEAL to rejoice in here, and most of it can be traced back to the willingness of so many citizens strange and even hostile to each other to sit down and talk candidly. Candor is a polite term for the blunt, sometimes harsh and bruising exchanges I listened to at planning sessions during the spring at Hiram House Camp. Under the patient and generous-spirited leadership of Dean Ostrum, chairman of the Council, those rough talk sessions bore real fruit. Not enough fruit yet—and no one recognizes that more keenly than Mr. Ostrum. Of the inner city's estimated 58,000 kids, probably only about 35,000 were served this summer. One high-risk project has already come to grief. There will be setbacks and disappointments in others. I hope Mr. Ostrum's 54 fat cats, do-gooders and young rebels will stick it out—for the sake of all of us.

APPENDIX #4
THEATRE LETTERS
"NOISES OFF" (Dean as Selsdon Mowbray) Mill Mountain Theatre, Roanoke, Virginia
Opening night notes from fellow actors:
Dear Dean, Have a great show tonight. It's been so nice to meet and work with you. Thanks for being such a sweety. You're a real gem. PATTY (Patricia Raun playing Belinda Blair) Dean: You're on! Break a leg! I'm very glad you were able to do the show. It's yours now—enjoy it fully. Best wishes,
JERE (Jere Lee Hodgin, Director)

Selsdon from Freddie, I don't know about you, but this is how I feel every night after doing the show (Paris photo of exhausted mongrel dog). But what a grand experience. And I feel like I've made a wonderful friend in Dean Ostrum. (unsigned card from Frank Roberts playing Frederick Fellowes) Dean—You sure got what it takes. Happy we've had a chance to work together and look forward to it again some day. Breaka leg Noises Off. DOTTY (Barbara Evans playing Dotty Otley)

Dear Dean—It's not many actors I've worked with who've dropped their pants for me twice each performance! Your Selsdon is a joy! Break-a-leg RACHEL (Rachel Sailer playing Poppy Norton-Taylor)

Excerpts from Terence Samuel REVIEW in Roanoke Times & World News:
The cast, overall, does an admirable job. Frank Roberts and Patricia Raun are outstanding. Roberts, who lives in

Tallahassee, Fla., plays Freddie Fellowes, an anxious, insecure, slightly phobic actor whose wife has left him on the day of the last rehearsal. Whenever Roberts takes the stage, though, there is laughter, and he is so innocently but persistently silly that just looking at him makes for a joke. Pat Raun plays Belinda Blair, a darling of a gossip who calls everybody "my sweet" as she slyly allows what she knows to go forth.

Dean Ostrum plays with a consistent, if not authentic accent. Ostrum plays an aging, imbibing actor who has very little grasp on the world about him, and he does it with a sensitivity and open bewilderment that will endear him to an audience. Laugher is the true test of a play like this—and this production just might ace it.

"THE SACRIFICIAL MURDERS OF MAINE VIRGINS FOR THE SAKE OF ART" Dean playing three roles—Minister, Art Patron, and Audience Member #2 (The Vortex Theater Company, New York City.

Dean,

Thanks so much for the help with the set and the food and the positive input. You've developed three hilarious characters which add a lot to the production.

DAVID (Writer and Director David Steinhart)

Dean,

You keep bringing flowers to us, and I wanted to bring some (written on card with flowers) to you. I would like to tell you what a wonderful human being you are. Always upbeat, looking at the positive of life. I like being around you. The AIDS work you do is emotionally hard, but I think it's wonderful that you care so much. I have loved working with you "on the boards". Thank you for your smiles and happiness.

Love DEB (actress Deb Snyder playing Monica Schneck)

"CAMPING WITH HENRY AND TOM" (Dean as "Thomas

Alva Edison")
Letter from professional actress Maeve McGuire after seeing the show:
A belated note to thank you again for such a splendid evening at The Comedy Club. I think it's the first time I've ever seen you on stage and I thought you were terrific. It's a mad and marvelous play and you were mad and marvelous!
Again-our thanks-love-hugs
MAEVE & RICHARD

"SOME ASSEMBLY REQUIRED" (Dean as "Dad")
Letter from Cecile Nebel, my French professor at Hunter College:
Cher Dean:
Mercei de m'avoer invitee a vener voir Some Assembly Required. Je suis totalement eblouie par votre magnifique talent que je n'avais pas soupconne. Votre energie, votre dynamesme et votre sens des nuances sont remarquables. Vous etes maintenant mon acteur prefere et je ne penserai plus jamais a Charlton Heston, car vous avez pres sa place dans mon estime.
Merci encore pour cette formidable après-medi.
Meilleures amities, CECILE

Note from two friends:
Thank you again for inviting us to your performance. It was very funny and we had a great time! It was great seeing you as "Dad", as well as the rest of the terrific cast. I hope to see you again soon, JEREMY & GEOFF

Note from the Director Stephen Willems:
"Dean—Thanks so much for your commitment and cute performance.
STEPHEN

Note from Plainfield, NJ, friends who collect my partner Richard's paintings:

"Dear Dean, Thanks again for the invitation to see Some Assembly Required last Saturday afternoon. What a wild bunch of characters—it must have been great fun playing those roles. And lots of dialogue; a lot to learn in so short a time. Hope you had as much fun acting as we did watching. Hope to see you and Richard again soon.
Sincerely,
PETER SIMONE & PAUL CHAPIN

E-mail from fellow professional actor who played Henry Ford opposite my Thomas Edison in "Camping with Henry and Tom":
Dear Dean,
While I asked Reed to pass on my praise for the production of "Some Assembly" and for your splendid performance— I'd like to be sure you know how much I enjoyed your work. You have a wonderful reality on stage and a very accurate sense of humor. Congratulations!
ED FRANKLIN

Opening Night note from professional actress CYD McDOWELL who played my daughter Stacy:
Daddy! I have loved every minute we have laughed and hugged and worked together. You are so funny and such a pro—I'm looking forward to a joyful and hilarious run.
Love and Kisses, STACY

APPENDIX #5
Letters Received When Departing Cleveland

The move to New York necessitated resigning from several civic posts as well as preparing an application for admission to the New York State Bar. Leaving Cleveland was likewise hard for Sari. Letters we received when the announcement of our move appeared in the press on March 15, 1974, are testimony to the place we had made for ourselves in the Greater Cleveland community. I include some of them, below. The first is from Newman T. Halvorson, a partner in

Ernst & Ernst and my successor as President of The Cleveland Museum of Natural History.

Dear Dean,

The announcement in Wednesday's papers was surely a shocker, at least to me. I congratulate you, and AT&T, but with regret for those of us who are left in Cleveland. It's no exaggeration to say that in this case the removal of one man will greatly decimate the forces for good in this community. I'm leaving this afternoon for Florida for a few weeks, so I may not see you before you leave.

All the best to you and Sari.

Newt

This from Lolette Hanserd, Associate Director of Cleveland Federation of Community Planning whose Executive Director Leona Bevis had made me chair of their Anti-social Gang Group Formation Study following the Hough Riots.

Dear Dean,

It was with very mixed emotions that I learned through our daily papers of you new position. First of all, however, let me extend congratulations to you, as well as best wishes, for happiness, success, and great satisfaction in your new endeavors and new home community. Secondly, let me say that my mixed reactions were due to my sincere regret that we can no longer have the benefit of your wise, compassionate, and vital leadership efforts in so many segments of the life of the Greater Cleveland community. It has been a real privilege for me to have worked with you in your various capacities with the former Welfare Federation and present Federation for Community Planning. I for one will miss your enthusiastic and intensive involvement. I do recognize, of course, that many of the contributions which you have made have helped push our community forward and will stand upon which we can continue even greater efforts. May I also extend my best wishes to your family as all of you meet the challenges of meeting new friends and becoming engaged in new pursuits.

Sincerely yours,

Lolette

The next is from Mrs. John A. "Lainie" Hadden, Jr. who succeeded me as Chair of the Board of Overseers of Case Western Reserve University (her handwritten notes on a formal letter inviting me to attend the fall meeting of the board where my past service was to be recognized).
We don't expect you – but there's no one we'd rather see.
Cordially [crossed out] With love to you & Sari.

Dean, I think of you and your splendid trail-blazing so often in this job. Indeed, there were so many areas blessed by your zest in Cleveland that I find myself thinking of you constantly and like your thousands of friends here, missing you greatly.

And this from Bruce H. Akers, a stockbroker, with whom I served in raising funds for the Big Brothers organization.
Dean,
I shall miss you. As I reflect on the years since I met you, I recall many pleasant occasions and visits with you. You have that rare quality of being a truly professional man and businessman, and yet possessing a great deal of humility and compassion for all walks of life. I only wish that I could have had the pleasure of visiting with you more often. Dean, you will be sorely missed in this community. Again my congratulations, and my best wishes to you. Mary Beth joins me in sending our regards to you and Sari.
Cordially,
Bruce

And this from Robert S. Oelman, Chairman of the National Cash Register Company in Dayton and an Ohio Bell board member.
Dear Dean: It was with mixed feelings that I heard of your resignation from Ohio Bell to accept the appointment with Western Electric in New York. You have done an outstanding job for Ohio Bell. Because of a schedule conflict I am sorry indeed that Mrs. Oelman and I cannot attend the dinner that

Fred is giving for you and Mrs. Ostrum. I did want you to know the reason why we will not be on hand in Cleveland that evening to join the others in giving you a warm sendoff.
With kindest personal regards,
Bob

And this from W. J. De Lancey, President of Republic Steel Corporation.
Dear Dean,
Undoubtedly I won't be the first to say it, but – The announcement of your advance into Western Electric does create a mixed reaction: We are delighted for you – it's not surprising that this recognition is forthcoming – but we regret that it means you will be leaving Cleveland.
Yours sincerely,
Bill

And this from Andrew L. Johnson, Jr. a black attorney friend.
Dear Dean,
I am indeed sorry to learn that you will be leaving us. I am sure that your move to New York City represents a well-deserved promotion. It has been a great pleasure to have known you in your many capacities and to have had the privilege of serving with you as a Trustee of the Bar Association of Greater Cleveland. I wish both you and your family great success and satisfaction in your new location. Let's keep in touch.
Very truly yours,
Andy

And this from Estal E. Sparlin, Governmental Management Consultant.
Dear Dean,
So the kid from Russell, Kansas, has another promotion. It is too bad your father cannot witness the results of his guidance of a wonderful son but I am sure your mother is very proud of you. I presume this means you will be moving to New York and that is a great loss to Greater Cleveland and Ohio. You

have been an inspiration to me and I am most grateful to you. I hope there will be more occasions when our paths cross.
Best wishes,
Estal

And from Louis A. Toepfer, President of Case Western Reserve University.
Dear Dean,
Bittersweet news it is. Happy for you, sad for us and Cleveland. Good luck and much happiness at Western Electric – that's our wish for you and your family.
Yours,
Louis

And this from Robert M. Ginn, President of the Cleveland Illuminating Co.
Dear Dean,
Congratulations on a promotion which sounds like a great step forward for you but certainly isn't for the City of Cleveland. While Ohio Bell people have always contributed to community betterment, and I am sure your successor will also, your contributions have been something special. Not only have your publicized jobs been significant but the unsung support in projects that were often controversial and too tough for others, and your wise counsel will be irreplaceable. You and Sari certainly leave with the best wishes of the entire community.
Sincerely,
Bob

And this from A. A. Sommer, Jr., a prominent Cleveland lawyer and former President of the Cleveland Welfare Association, then in Washington, D.C.
Dear Dean,
I was both dismayed and delighted to learn that you are moving to New York and increased responsibilities and position. I think this is great for Western Electric and the Bell

System, but I think it is a grievous loss for the Cleveland community.

Dean, you were one of the really solid rocks in Cleveland. I think only those of us who were deeply involved in community activities really had a full perception of all you accomplished and how much you meant to the city. One of my great pleasures in my activities was the chance to be associated with you. Starr [his wife] joins in sending our very best to you, Sari and your family for every success and happiness in New York. And congratulations on this move. It is obviously a clear recognition of the abilities you brought not only to the matters in which we were involved, but to your legal endeavors as well.

Sincerely,

Al

And from David Arnold, whose company specialized in management consulting and executive selection, and who was also our neighbor in Waite Hill Village.

Dear Dean,

Congratulations on your appointment as Vice President, Western Electric Company. I read this news with mixed emotions. The position will offer new challenge, professional horizons, and New York will feed your appetite for culture, organization, and people. However, the riding stables may be miles away. Cleveland will miss your friendliness, leadership, and personal vibrancy, which have contributed to enriching the quality of life here. Carol and I wish you and your family good luck. An old Irish blessing best expresses our feelings:

May the road rise to meet you,
May the wind be always at your back.
May the sun shine warm upon your face,
The rain fall soft upon your fields.
And until we meet again,
May God hold you in the palm of his hand.

And lastly, a hand-written letter from W. T. McCullough, Cleveland Welfare Association Executive, who was instrumental in having Mayor Carl Stokes designate me Chairman of the Mayor's Council on Youth Opportunity.

Dear Dean,

I've been afraid I'd read a story such as the attached someday and here it is. Dean, it has been wonderful to be associated with you over the past 12 years. I can remember the first time I met you – on East Ninth and Prospect, with Penny Pendleton. Since then my years have been enriched by the privilege to work with you. You have always taken time to learn about problems of the community which were not yours except as you made them yours. We've got problems in our country, but in due course they will be dealt with constructively because of people like you. And the Cleveland community is better because you were here. We'll miss you greatly, but I'll add my good wishes to you and Sari, and your family, for the years ahead. We'll hope to keep in touch. The best of success and satisfaction to you.

Sincerely,

Tom

APPENDIX #6

While I chose not to follow the custom of having a Memory Book on retirement from the Bell System, I did receive a few notes that meant a lot to me.

Mr. Ostrum,

Working for you has been the highlight of my career. Tom and I wish you great success in your new career, good times, good health, and much happiness.

Marion (Marion Ellis, my personal secretary during all my years in New York)

Dear Mr. Ostrum,

How difficult to tell you how very much I have enjoyed working with you these past years. There are no words, clichés, phrases, etc., which could ever express my true feelings. I have truly enjoyed those years. Your constant

cheerfulness and enthusiasm is so prominent as I recall our day-to-day contacts. Always a smile and a feeling of warmth.
Adieu, dear friend. I wish you all the best in your retired life.
I know you are deeply involved in your second love and that you will find much happiness in being able to devote your time to such a worthy second career.
Thank you, thank you again for everything.
Fondly, Dorothy (Dorothy Crowe, the personal secretary to both my bosses while at Western Electric in New York)

Dear Dean,

I am truly sorry that the AT&T Seminar prevents me from attending the farewell gathering in your honor. It is truly symbolic, I believe of the "new age" in which we live at AT&T. Yet, being away, I have all the greater incentive to speak from the heart in a way that I perhaps could not do as well face to face, since we still are so much constrained to limit ourselves to so-called "manly sentiments".

We have shared much together professionally. We have played major roles in the most exciting period in AT&T's history— looked at, at least, from the legal viewpoint. I have flourished, I think, and functioned, at the best I could deliver in large part because of the encouragement, support, and friendship you brought to every day's problems and situations.

I will always value and seek to emulate your patience, gentleness, and good judgment in matters of the heart and mind. As one who is very interested in theater, I suspect that these qualities will stand you well in your effort to continually deepen your characterization of different personalities on the stage.

Meri and I wish you the very best future you can ask for: a future of good health, of artistic accomplishment and recognition—and reward, of emotional fulfillment in every way. You and George, as you leave, beckon to me to do the same, when I can. You seem to say, "fight the good fight, and when the job is done, it is time to move on!" I hear you. May God bless you and always be attentive to you.

Sincerely, Lippman (one of my top staff attorneys, Lippman Bodoff)

Dear Dean,
Since you have decided not to have a memory book, I am taking the liberty of writing you a brief note to express to you the respect and friendship I have for you. I can remember hearing about the dynamic Kansan who was rising through the Bell System when I first came with Southwestern Bell over 25 years ago. I doubt if anyone has equaled your record of being a Vice President, General Counsel of two operating companies, and when you add your most recent position, your accomplishments are most impressive. But of equal or greater importance is the fact that you have always conducted yourself with integrity, thoughtfulness and as a consummate gentleman. We will miss you, look forward to seeing you on stage and screen in the not too distant future and hope that we will continue to see you from time to time as your vocation changes, but, hopefully, not your friends. Katie sends her best regards and wishes for a happy and successful second career.
Sincerely, Jim (James A. DeBois, highranking AT&T attorney)

Dear Dean,
I learned of your retirement in Washington, D.C. in recent days. It seems hard to believe to say the least! It seems like yesterday when you asked me to come and work for you at Ohio Bell. I worked for many fine men but you were and are the very-very best, Dean. I am most grateful to you as is Jeanne and the children.

My office in Kansas City is, and always has been patterned on your management style. That's the finest tribute I can pay you. Dean, Jeanne joins me in wishing you the best that our hearts can imagine for you. Our very best holiday wishes to you and your lovely family.
Most sincerely,
Clark (Clark Redick, AT&T General Attorney)

REMARK OF GEORGE V. COOK AT THE OFFICER RETIREMENT DINNER GIVEN FOR DEAN:
We gather here tonight to honor one of our colleagues on his retirement after more than three decades with the Bell System. He is a class individual. He personifies that unique mixture of competence, civility and decency with an overriding concern for people. What greater compliment could be paid to him than Ernie Gleit did last night when he characterized Dean as the perfect boss. (George Cook was Dean's boss and Ernie Gleit was one of Dean's lawyers.)

ACKNOWLEDGEMENTS

Thanks first to my son John Ostrum for suggesting decades ago that I write about my life—both of us aware that the day would come when I'd no longer be around to answer his questions. I wished that my father had done so and it seemed like a good idea. But procrastination soon followed and it wasn't until I began auditing French classes at Hunter College in New York that I noticed a summer course in Advanced Expository Writing. I took the course and thanks to the editors of the college literary journal "The Olive Tree", a piece I had written was chosen for publication and I experienced the thrill of becoming a "published writer"—barely, that is, but one all the same. Much of the final chapter in this book originated with that effort. Again procrastination followed and only after receiving encouragement from my dear friend Mollie McGreevy, an associate priest at the Greenwich Village Church of St. Luke's in the Fields did I begin again. She found the first version of my chapter "Outed by My Children" of compelling interest and told me that my writing might be of great benefit to gay men struggling with their identity and others in straight society as well. With urging from my partner Richard Nagrodsky I began to write in earnest and found additional encouragement from my close friend Catherine Maldonaldo who in her late nineties had privately published a delightful book about her early life entitled "The Malvern Stories". Through my beloved Catherine (who peacefully died just three days after we shared high tea together in her home) I met Melody Lawrence and her professional services have been indispensable in bringing this writing effort to a conclusion.

Special thanks go to each of my four children—Karna, John, Daniel, and Peter—for their writings about what it has meant to have a gay father, and also to my loving, former wife Sari for sharing the trove of love letters I wrote to her during the several years of the two wars that separated us.

Finally I thank my partner of almost thirty-two years, Richard, for his continuing encouragement to keep going and great patience when procrastination threatened to end this project before completion.